The Sacred Sequence
Remembering the One Truth

John J. Burton, EdD

JCP

Jan-Carol
Publishing, Inc

"every story needs a book"

The Sacred Sequence
Remembering the One Truth
John J. Burton, EdD

Published May 2017
Express Editions
Imprint of Jan-Carol Publishing, Inc
All rights reserved
Copyright © 2017 by John J. Burton, EdD

ISBN: 978-1-945619-28-1
Library of Congress Control Number: 2017943260

You may contact the publisher:
Jan-Carol Publishing, Inc
PO Box 701
Johnson City, TN 37605
publisher@jancarolpublishing.com
jancarolpublishing.com

There are many thanks and appreciations to express for all that manifested into this book. First and last, I want to thank the One who makes all things possible; I am forever honored and grateful for the infinite generosity and love that is. I extend thanks to my clients, who honored me with their trust and taught me so much about life and love. Thanks to my many teachers for supporting me, and sharing their wisdom and love. I thank my wife, Irene, for endless support and encouragement. Her devotion, ever-willing, heart, wisdom and love, provide priceless contributions to this book and my life. Thank you for the gift of you. Thanks to friends who tolerated my frustrations and joys along the way while writing this book. I want to express appreciation to Michael and Holly for their kind contributions of time, wisdom, and heart. I thank my editors, Shanna and Catherine, for their wonderful insights and the skills to help bring this material to completed form.

To the Reader

First, thank you for choosing to read, explore and journey with the material of this book. I hope the experience provides new insights and assists in your own awakening as the clarity of these truths have provided this for me. It is in the spirit of compassion and Grace that I invite you to read and re-connect with your eternal self to remember the One Truth of your being, your unity with Creator, your being as an extension of God and all that this Truth provides. I am grateful to have received this material from Spirit and it is my privilege to share it with you.

Enjoy your journey toward wholeness,
John Burton

Prologue

I believe we each experience a series of awakenings throughout our lifetimes. Some of these awakenings come in the midst of dark times, while others come during a period of clear open-mindedness or joy. My lifelong quest to understand human nature begins with what I consider to be my first awakening, when I was thirteen years old.

My eighth-grade science textbook included a chapter on psychology. In this chapter, there were half a dozen or so vignettes describing people's thoughts, emotions, and behaviors. I was instantly hooked. I read the chapter over and over, because I wanted to understand what makes us think, feel, and behave the way we do. My search for answers continues to this day.

I now work as a licensed counselor, with a doctorate in human development counseling and several professional certifications. I have gained the benefits of much training and many mentors, along with my nearly 35 years of experience working with clients who have taught me a great deal about human nature. From this collective experience, I have come to discover and understand some things about how and why we do as we do.

The result of these awakenings, or sudden expanded awareness, is that our consciousness reaches a higher level and our awareness expands; we feel better, and we live better. Sometimes we seek these awareness-expanding experiences; sometimes they find us. While I grow as a person from my own expanding awareness, sharing this with others is what really makes the process valuable. In this book, I share with you my current consciousness and awareness of human nature in the hope that it will contribute to your own awakening.

The roots of this book extend back about twelve years, to a dream that came to me one night. I was out of town and out of my routines, which so often creates an opening for new communication with Divine Spirit. So it was that night. This dream came to me in the form of a trilogy: one dream with three parts. I present to you the results of the dream and what it set in motion, which guided me from my illusions back to the sacred sequence and the One Truth. Further, while the dream presented many rich symbols and guidance, I believe these symbols to be universal, with applications to us all.

In this dream, which I'll detail more in Chapter 1, I was told of an arrangement—a sequence of sacred energy that allows our optimal free being. This Sacred Sequence, as I have since come to name it, consists of faith, hope, love, and charity applied to God, self, others, and the universe in this order. In this context, *God* means the all-loving Divine Source that provides a constant presence of our love-worthiness. A powerful freeing element in the sequence is that we come to remember the Creator as the Source of our constant worth. This removes the humans and possessions from Source, freeing us from the illusion that someone or something else provides our love-worthiness.

I spent the next twelve years after this dream identifying the pieces that precede the solution—the disarray that makes the solution necessary. My professional development, experience, and personal development have allowed me a firsthand glimpse into the human processes that lead us astray from the Sacred Sequence. This book combines what I have learned over these years with what I was told that one night, twelve years ago.

One of the essential aspects in wellbeing that I came to realize after this dream is what I refer to as the One Truth. There exists a state of consciousness, described by many Eastern religions and philosophers, in which we experience unity with God. Please insert whatever term you prefer for God, this nameless, frameless, infinite, eternal, all-loving energy of the universe. In this experience of unity, each person discovers a clean, pure sense of self—or perhaps an absence of self—devoid of the accumulated human misconceptions. It seems that all cultures make reference to this state, yet we easily lose sight of it.

The One Truth is what you experience in this unity, and what you come to know about your being. You are love: this is your eternal essence that never wavers, no matter what you do, because it is your very being. Forgetting this Truth happens in response to emotional trauma, which then leads us to make desperate efforts to regain this feeling of lost love. Poor choices made from our survival-based human self and further loss of self-worth follow.

In this book, we explore how we forget and how we can remember, aligning with the Sacred Sequence as a way back to the One Truth. Living from this One Truth allows us to express our gifts freely, enhancing ourselves and others in the process.

The progression of this book starts with what I call the fundamental error, then retraces our misguided steps back to our point of true being. Each of us experiences some type and degree of emotional trauma in this life, which represents the human condition and challenge. We quickly believe that trauma is the event, in what amounts to a mental reflex of our survival brain. But the effects of trauma are more about our response than the event itself. It's just that our primitive, survival brain and its exclusively external focus sees the trauma as the source of our distress, rather than our internal response. I use the term primitive brain, but it has many aliases: ego-self, monkey mind, left brain, etc.

This response of focusing on the event and resulting beliefs separates us from the Sacred Sequence and One Truth, preventing us from healing. Trauma is a *response* to an event, not the event. This focus on our responses is true for other incidents as well, not just traumatic ones. The life we experience greatly stems from the consequences of our responses. Due to this fact, we can access our inner responses to bring healing. This book also illustrates ways to access your own trauma responses, stop criticism of the self, end self-defeating loops, reclaim lost parts of the self, and realize you are "good enough," allowing you to live from a place of experiencing and sharing your love-worthiness.

In addition to the Sacred Sequence and the One Truth, you will see some other terms along the way of this journey to your Truth. This includes the primitive brain.

This part of the self equates to our limbic system—the fight, flight, or freeze response. It also refers to our ego, left brain, and the part of the self that automatically interprets and responds to traumatic events in life.

You'll also see the term *backward logic*. This is what I call the type of reasoning used by the primitive brain. It is the opposite of the Sacred Sequence's spiritual logic, in which our love-worthiness originates from Creator and remains eternal.

Our primitive brain believes that what happens outside of the self determines what happens inside of the self. From this perspective, our emotions, beliefs about God, self, life, and others are determined by external events, spawning countless illusions. A rather helpless, adversarial relationship then develops between the self and the outside world.

With the basic elements and challenges outlined here, where do we begin this process of remembering the One Truth?

In order to get where we want to go, we have to start where we are. The chapters in this book are purposely designed in an order that allows our whole being to reach and experience the Sacred Sequence and One Truth—not just the part of us that is unencumbered, able to reach oneness easily. Too often we focus on the parts of ourselves that are fully functional, and neglect or even reject aspects of the self that appear deficient. This Sequence and Truth are intended for all of you, every part, especially the treasures imbedded within those rejected parts.

It seems that we each experience a compelling drive to overcome the inevitable emotional traumas of this life, in order to live our true abilities. As Spirit once spoke these inspiring words to me, *Our deepest dreams never die; we are either planning, pursuing, or attempting to resist their incessant beckoning.* Experiencing the One Truth not only answers all questions about our true being, but also, more profoundly, mutes all questions of self-worth.

In the process of reading and experiencing the material in this book, you will discover unique understandings about your self, forgiveness, and spiritual relations.

You will be guided through powerful exercises to assist you in reclaiming lost parts of the self, and bringing healing love to restore the Sacred Sequence so you can remember your own Truth. These tried and true effective exercises, tools, and skills will remain with you into your future, so that you will possess a collection of ways to either prevent or overcome emotional trauma, free to live and share the One Truth.

This book escorts you on a journey away from the illusions created by our primitive brain, guiding you to reach the Sacred Sequence so that you can experience and live from your One Truth. It is not designed just for your head; it guides you into your heart, toward Divine love. We'll begin this journey at the outermost conscious layer. No judging—just digging, discovering, and understanding along the way to the Sacred Sequence and the One Truth. This leads us on a unique path that will yield new awareness and the original you!

Table of Contents

CHAPTER 1

THE ESSENTIAL
INGREDIENTS

How do you get to the Truth and experience it? You dig through the layers of illusions to remember your essence of pure love. In the process of passing through the layers of illusions, you may uncover some frustrating loops in your life, and break free from self-defeating choices. You will come to find that these counterproductive ways provide the very opportunities you seek to reclaim your Sacred Self.

During this trek, you may find that you encounter forms of self-criticism and discover the roots of these, releasing the effects of past emotional traumas. You can identify and gain release from old patterns that led you into unsatisfying relationships with the same type of person. No judging allowed, just interpreting and understanding what you find.

Along your path, you will come across a different way to understand forgiveness that assists you in reclaiming your true self and the freedom you desire. New abilities will become available, empowering you by developing skills that transform self-criticism and unjust restrictions, permitting you to rise above the effects of past emotional trauma. You can discover and experience a healthy love and deep appreciation of the self as you find that you *are* the person you always wanted to become.

Your very being is of love, of the One Source; no human gave it to you, nor can anyone take it away. This is the One Truth. You are this before your first breath. In a way, we are becoming what we already are: love.

I invite you to join me as we begin this trek back along the stepping-stones of the Sacred Sequence, returning to the One Truth.

As noted in the Prologue, the roots of this book extend back about twelve years to a dream that came to me one night. I was out of town and out of my routines, which so often creates an opening for new communication with Divine Spirit. So it was that night. This dream came to me in the form of a trilogy—one dream with three parts. The result of the dream is what I present to you now in this book, which guided me from my illusions back to the Sacred Sequence and the One Truth.

The first part of the trilogy takes place in an unknown house. I stand inside a house with an unidentified man, looking out through a large window at the surrounding countryside. This man was known as a very skeptical person—difficult to reason with, and doubtful of anything beyond his own thoughts and beliefs. The skeptical one is totally convinced that a civil war rages in the surrounding countryside. I know for sure that no fighting exists, but I also know that trying to talk him out of his belief is useless.

While gazing out through the window, we suddenly see a massive explosion in the distance. A huge fireball billows up into the air; several more explosions follow. I realize that this explosion reveals the unfolding of an ingenious scheme. The only way to change this skeptic's position is by acknowledging his belief that a civil war actually exists. So, in this dream, someone creates the illusion of blowing up the rebel's ammunition dump. Now, with no ammunition left that could be used to fight the war, the war ends, and he knows it—one illusion serves to dispel another.

The dream instantly shifts scenes, beginning the second part of the trilogy. I was sitting at a small table in a sidewalk café. The house and skeptic are gone, replaced by the very pleasant outdoor café setting, where I then meet an unknown woman. She sits down at the table next to mine, holding a bag or a satchel of sorts.

The woman leans over toward me and hands me the satchel, which contains a book. I did not see the book; I could only feel it in the bag and know it is in there. As she hands me the book bag, she says, "I'm not sure if you will write it." Poof–scene two ends, and the dream moves to scene three in a seamless yet abrupt manner.

The third dream sequence opens with me standing next to a rather short man resembling the Wizard in *The Wizard of Oz*. This short, well-dressed man proceeds to tell me about the machinery and grid system that surrounded us. As he explained, I expressed my amazement for this vast, intricate system. He humbly informs me that it was just a little something he put together.

"This system just *is*," he tells me, "like numbers simply exist–never right or wrong." He suggests the following to me, as an example.

"Take the number four. It just is, and is never right or wrong. And then you can take four times four."

I wondered the purpose for his suggestion, and asked, "What's four times four?"

He replied, "Sick teens."

I had to laugh and yet was stunned at the same time. Sick teens?!

This wizard, who I sense is some embodiment of Divine Spirit, goes on to tell me about four times four. He says that four times four means faith, hope, love, and charity toward God, self, others, and the universe.

It struck me that these particular qualities in this particular order seems to comprise some sort of sequence for wellbeing–a Sacred Sequence.

Now, what would I do with what feels like such vital information? Four times four equals sick teens? What in the world? Well, I know that sixteen represents an age at which we expand our earlier life experiences and beliefs out into the larger world. So, whatever our belief foundation may be, especially formed in our family of origin, tends to become the perspective we often rely on and project onto the world around us.

Some of the dream symbols also hold particular meaning, and not just for me. The skeptic at the window with me seems to represent the primitive brain, its lack of trust, and chronic skepticism. We each have one of these inner skeptics. The civil war in the dream is the war that sometimes rages within the self. We each experience the battle between those two factions of perspectives and beliefs that fight for supremacy—the negative voice and the positive voice, left brain and right brain, or Spirit-self and ego-self.

As we will come to find out later in our journey, the presence of the illusions created by the primitive brain represents a significant hurdle to overcome in our process of healing self. In a way, healing means dissolving our self-created illusions—and thus, their consequences. In the dream, the skeptic holds illusions that the war is real. However, we can't just let our Spirit-self tell our skeptic, "Oh, you're just mistaken; there's no war happening." The skeptic would not believe the spirit. To reconcile and dispel the illusions, we must treat them as real and then arrange ways to diffuse and nullify them. We work in the realm of illusions in order to gain release, using one illusion to dissolve another. This book provides numerous exercises that assist you in illusion busting.

And finally, although we could evaluate most dreams for a long time, always finding more information, let's look at the wizard character. His very presence reveals a major truth. In the movie *The Wizard of Oz*, we find that all the characters eventually realize on their journey to Oz that they already possess the qualities they desire.

So, this dream also conveys the unspoken message that we each already have just what we desire, within us. We are already the person we always wanted to be; we just need to uncover, reclaim, and allow this emergence. And you are the one who performs the process in and for yourself.

While unraveling the messages of this dream, I continued working with clients in my counseling practice. I recognized how we respond to trauma by turning the offender into some sort of all-powerful being who determines our self-worth. We also rely on our primitive brain, our least able aspect of the self,

4

for decisions about daily living.

It has long been known that a state of consciousness exists that accesses a sense of unity with God: God consciousness, as it is sometimes called. Many spiritualists and mystics—from Buddha to Christ to Trungpa, Ken Wilbur, James Finley, Thomas Merton, Meister Eckhart, Alan Watts, and others—speak of this consciousness. This highest state led me to recognize what I now call the One Truth. In unity with God or Source, we recognize our innate, eternal worth that precedes our human birth. This Truth provides us with a liberating perspective about ourselves and our life events.

It is here in the place of unity that we each realize this One Truth. We exist within this infinite, eternal love, and actually consist of this energy. All doubts about self-worth and love-worthiness vanish. This One Truth replaces all, as it *is* All. We then learn to live from this awareness and its amazing properties in life as a human, a little more every day. I suggest that every act we choose is designed to either *connect with* the Divine, or *maintain* this connection.

The core issue that interferes with remembering this One Truth for each of us is emotional trauma and our reaction to it. Every individual experiences childhood trauma to some degree, and such emotional upset just seems to be an inevitable part of life. The only tool we have available in childhood to make sense of this trauma is the ill-formed logic of a child. Additionally, our primitive brain kicks in, even in adulthood in response to emotional trauma, impairing our ability to interpret events.

As a result of this limited reasoning ability that personalizes everything, the child often ends up feeling like he or she *caused* the trauma and is therefore deserving of the mistreatment received. It may also include forming some self-condemning beliefs, including doubts about being worthy of love. In this same way, a child then also forms misconceptions about God, relationships, life, and how the Divine works. The post-traumatic impact is that we form our self-concept and belief system based on the trauma, instead of remembering our pre-existing love-worthiness.

The reasoning abilities of the brain in childhood lead us to believe that some other person—the trauma inflictor, or those of a similar style—is our life source, and can keep us alive or exterminate us. Just look at the power displayed by the offender as seen through the eyes of an innocent child. This places the offender in the god role. We then use other forms of limited thinking, which comprises our survival mode or primitive brain. This results in seeing others as our source of love-worthiness.

We try to extract redemption and love-worthiness from the offender, or those like the offender, through our behavior and accomplishments. Brief and fleeting success may happen, but the results fade quickly because nothing external lasts. We try to convert any success into a sense that we are worthy of love. Based on this feat, we then hope that somehow God will deem us worthy of love.

In the meantime, this primitive-brain reasoning has decided that God resembles the offender from childhood—unreliable, fickle, judging, and mostly rejecting and condemning. The Sequence loses the sacredness, becoming out of order—starting with an all-or-nothing, life-or-death emphasis on others, then proceeding to self, God, and the universe.

Using this sort of reasoning, we function from a place of misunderstanding as we venture out into the larger world. We live believing the one truth is that we are not worthy of love, and we search for how can we make up for this. We live based on inaccurate beliefs about God, self, others, and the universe, creating various forms of sickness, disease, or dysfunction in our inner self and our lives.

The post-trauma assumption is that we are somehow inferior and unworthy, so we must urgently search for a way to correct our unworthy selves. The solution, then, is to restore this original Divine arrangement of faith, hope, love, and charity toward God, self, others and the universe. The result is streaming love-worthiness. This sequence allows us to remember our aboriginal and eternal love-worthiness. This sacred principle forms a sort of relationship between the four qualities and the four recipients, a four-by-four relationship.

Let me show you with a brief example: Most of us have encountered a bridge along our life path that tells us we are not "good enough." I know I have crossed this bridge several times, and it tends to appear when I want to accomplish something. I don't know about out you, but I never get an answer when I ask that voice, "I'm not good enough for what?"

I do know that the voice comes from earlier life experiences, and it asks me to prove my worth. This voice displays the very misalignment of the primitive brain. It believes that I *may* gain my worth, *after* some accomplishment. This perspective reveals the out-of-order sequence of making others the sole priority. *Others* includes anything outside of the self (such as people, accomplishments, or possessions) that is supposedly convertible into others valuing us. We then attempt to negotiate the hurdles of self, God, and the universe. In this disorder, very little remains of faith, hope, love, or charity. Needs for survival are too strong to allow room for such vulnerability.

Now, what happens within the self when we apply the Sacred Sequence? We start with faith, hope, love, and charity toward God. With this we rediscover our innate worthiness, which we possessed before our first breath. From here, we apply the same four qualities to the self, then to others and the universe. Once the Sequence resumes, we find that there exists no such concept as good enough, because we already exist as good enough, for all eternity. This four-quality set applied to the four recipients creates a tightly-woven structure of four times four.

Furthermore, we don't expect infants to earn their worth, do we? At what age does the misconception come to life when we suddenly disregard our innate worth and our inner God, requiring *proof* of our worth? This is the fundamental error I refer to in the Prologue.

This fundamental error happens when we let our primitive brain decide the meaning of life events. The other part of this misalignment occurs when we let our survival brain choose our response strategy in life. Since our survival brain is fear-based, each option it considers is geared toward preventing loss. It overlooks the infinite source of love-worthiness already present in us and around us. It operates from a scarcity mentality.

This limited thinking and awareness leads to choices that actually *create* what we fear.

For example, a person may avoid interacting with other people to prevent being rejected and ending up alone. However, we end up alone by not interacting with others—an odd shortcut for sure! Each choice of life management from the primitive brain suffers from what I described earlier as backward logic. The primitive brain reverses both the source of self-worth and the effective solution. We do the exact opposite of what would help us in a given situation.

One of my clients reasons that if she lets out the years of pent up emotions they "will never end." However, the truth is that if she lets them out, they *will end*, and if she does not let them out, then they will not end. The reasoning and response strategy is completely backward. I liken this process to how we tend to treat leftovers in the refrigerator. The leftovers just keep getting pushed further and further to the back of the refrigerator until one day we open the refrigerator, and... Ugh, that stinks!

The primitive brain bases life decisions on the belief that things and people outside of us cause what we experience inside. The response then gears to a supposed outside source that holds our personal power and love-worthiness.

Once we come to believe the misunderstanding of our primitive brain, we start living from a place where we feel a loss of love-worthiness. Sadness, anxiety, and anger in various forms often accompany this feeling of loss. The next step is to compensate for this illusion, and attempt various feats in search of relief. These efforts just pull us further away from our inner love-worthiness, which waits for us to remember it.

The primitive brain thinks in finite, tangible terms. So it believes that the sources of the much sought-after feeling of love-worthiness are like food and water: in limited supply. Backtracking from the fundamental error and its ripple effects, we can recover lost parts of the self, and restore the Sacred Sequence to remember the One Truth.

As we explore our primitive brain a bit more closely, we find at least four core beliefs making up the operating system. These core beliefs are not all that comprise the primitive brain, but they strongly influence our thoughts, emotions, and behavior. These four core beliefs are listed below.

1. All valuable aspects of life are external; they are finite and temporary (the paradox in the mind created by trauma and fear).
2. The unwanted is permanent, while the positive is fleeting.
3. One either acquires the valuable things or does not, which creates emotional musical chairs.
4. Instant duality: Notice how it feels within if you believe that all power and valuables are external, finite, and temporary—and you either acquire them, or you don't.

These four traits, including duality, also instantly generate conceptual byproducts of fair, blame, and fault.

Judgment is another way the primitive brain tries to manage the illusions. Once we attempt to find our love-worthiness from an external source, it can only disappointment us. Then the primitive brain finds fault, blame, judgment, and similar reactions.

It's as if living from the primitive brain leads us to sort leftover scraps of energy, and we just don't know what to do with them or how to get rid of them. Furthermore, since we seek equilibrium by nature, we feel compelled to rid ourselves of the excess. There are no leftovers when living from the One.

Restoring the Sacred Sequence allows us to undo and remove the unnecessary painful illusions about ourselves. As we reverse the fallout of backward logic, we can stop manifesting our fears and begin manifesting Divine Spirit. We then naturally extend and express this infinite source of love toward others and our world. The result is faith, hope, love, and charity toward God, self, others, and the universe—returning you to the One Truth.

"Love is infallible; it has no errors for all errors are the want of love."
—William Law

CHAPTER 2

THE FUNDAMENTAL ERROR

There really exists just one Source of everyone and everything in this universe. This is the place of One Truth. The Source consists of pure love and infinite, eternal generosity. It is called God by some, the Great Spirit by others, and the One, as well as many other names in different cultures and traditions. This Source comprises our very makeup, our eternal essence.

However, when we come to this earth as humans, this life brings some sort of emotional trauma to us each. As noted earlier, it seems to be the human condition. This trauma leads to us forgetting our essence and the truth about our being because our primitive brain takes over, managing our life in response to trauma.

This forgetting opens the door to many ego-self generated illusions about ourselves and our lives. Emotional pain then follows, generating relentless efforts to compensate for these illusions so that we can remember the One Truth. Upon remembering the Truth, we find spontaneous transformation through profound awareness of this love. We'll also see how the Sacred Sequence allows us to remember the One Truth, reconnecting us with our fundamental love-worthiness.

The following example will help you to understand how we forget. It illustrates the way this primitive brain of ours plays out the fundamental error. Let's take the case of one of my clients.

"I know what I need to do," Caroline said in a calm and confident voice. A fifty-something educated professional who had experienced depression and anxiety most of her life, Caroline had broken free of her illusions, and begun reclaiming herself and creating her desired life. She let go of the painful judgments she'd received from others throughout her life. Caroline also stopped chasing some kind of absolution and sense of love-worthiness from outside herself. No longer striving for perfection and endless achievements, she now experiences Divine love from within, and expresses this in her unique ways. She knows she was, is, and always will be worthy of love.

This life-altering transformation happens by applying the Sacred Sequence: faith, hope, love, and charity toward God, self, others, and the universe. In order to experience the relief, let's start at the error, undo it, and then move forward.

What Caroline perceived in childhood was that her parents existed as all powerful, life-giving, *and potentially life-taking* deities. Caroline believed that her parents' criticism and judgment of her meant she was not worthy of love. She felt that she had lost her love-worthiness, and needed to find a way to get it back.

One way she could do this was by trying to win over her parents, or someone who reminded her of her parents. She might develop a relentless drive to achieve and acquire things which she could cash in for her love-worthiness. She could also combine these for "extra credit." In one way or another, most of us create a false deity that we serve in order to regain self-worth.

When we experience an emotional hurt or trauma, whether it's generated by our parents or some other significant person, we convert the offender into our god. It's also true that since we're human, we continue contending with the part of ourselves that actually believes our love-worthiness resides outside of us, and must be earned. However, we can use effective ways to override the illusions and make peace within ourselves.

How does this deity making happen? The process represents a reflex of our brain's limbic system, a response that you've probably heard of, called the fight, flight, or freeze reaction to stress. Yet this primitive part of our brain does so much more.

Our primitive left brain, which contains the limbic system, works from a particular style of reasoning that I'll detail shortly. For now, just know that our brain is restricted to this way of reasoning for about the first seven years of life. As a result, we can only process stressful or frightening events through our primitive brain. However, this part of us possesses the least ability for the job of interpreter.

This restricted reasoning style makes emotional trauma in childhood almost inevitable. However, emotional trauma can also occur in adulthood, as deeply felt emotional threats activate this primitive brain and its view of the world. General day-to-day life stress can also incite the limbic system's activation, and then it directs our perception and choices.

This ego-self inevitably generates an emotional wound and misconceptions about our love-worthiness that we carry with us into adolescence and adulthood. We long for love, yet feel unworthy of it! The human condition of anger, fear, and sadness resides here. The compensation efforts set in motion to obtain the missing love-worthiness only create additional problems because they don't address the misconception. They work with it as though it is valid!

This collection of illusions and compensating efforts brings us back to the illusion of the civil war that took place in my dream. The fight within ourselves—the debate about our worth—exists as the civil war in our head. We believe our emotional wounds are real, and our primitive brain can't just let go of them. Responding to the illusions as though they are real, let us metaphorically blow up the rebels' ammunition dump, ending the war. We do this by bringing the Sacred Sequence and One Truth to the wound.

We will identify and call on these advanced skills as we go along the path of reclaiming our love-worthiness.

Our primitive brain possesses a style of reasoning that sets us up for feeling unworthy of love. While useful as a physical survival mechanism, the primitive brain overreacts and oversteps its territory when we're faced with emotional trauma. Misconceptions inevitably form when the primitive brain tries to make sense of emotional trauma.

I'll detail the traits of the primitive brain in the next chapter, but for now, here's the gist.

Our ego-self (or at the physiological level, our left brain) believes everything that happens is about itself, and that it causes everything that happens. It also thinks that when any two events happen closely together in time, the first event causes the second.

You know the feeling; you walk into a room where a group of people is gathered. Right when you walk in, someone knocks over his or her coffee cup. For a moment, you may actually think you made this happen!

On a larger scale, this primitive brain can have us feeling responsible for someone else's behavior, believing we caused it—yet we are unable to control the other person. Good luck in getting that elusive person to show you love! It's not about you; you did not make the individual withhold love, and you can't *make* someone change. More importantly, no human is the source of another's love-worthiness.

Our left brain has some other interesting traits. It locks on to an issue or a point of view but can't sense beyond its narrow focus, believing what it senses is all that exists. Lacking the power of discernment, our primitive brain takes a single example and generalizes it to all similar instances.

For example, when an emotionally elusive person doesn't show you love, the primitive brain first believes that this elusive one is the *only* person who holds the love supply. Then, when eventually considering other potential love sources (other people), the primitive brain believes that they will naturally reject him as well.

This limbic brain also reasons solutions in a perfectly backward way. We'll let fictional "Jack" provide an example of how our primitive brain misinterprets things when faced with emotional trauma. Jack reports experiencing depression since early puberty. It turns out that Jack's mother was depressed as far back as he can remember.

Whenever young Jack started feeling happy and began breaking free in life to naturally explore, his mother would display more intense depression symptoms and ignore him. Self-sacrificing Jack could only gain his mother's "love" if he restricted himself. (The sociologist Margaret Mead called this the "re-approachment" phase of a young child's life.)

This restriction and self-denial led to Jack's sadness. His "deity-mother" conveyed that only through self-restriction and sadness could Jack become worthy of love, with her as the source. The reversed logic translated this as a need for him to deny his true self in order for his true self to be validated! Since he believed that his love-worthiness came from something or someone on this earth, he was then set up for a never-satisfying chase.

To reiterate, the Sacred Sequence reminds us of our love-worthiness by starting with God, the One Truth, and then applying this to self, others, and the universe. However, our primitive brain creates illusions and reverses this process. This backward process for obtaining love-worthiness, from others to self to God, sets in motion an array of love-deficit responses. Also, notice how this reversed process naturally leaves out the universe, leading to neglect or abuse of nature and animals.

In summary, starting from some original emotional trauma, our limbic brain takes over and we come to doubt our love-worthiness. Since the primitive brain believes that a human withheld our love, then surely this or some other human must have it to give to us. The illusions created by our primitive brain lead to symptoms of sadness, anxiety, and anger. We may take out these painful illusions and the emotions they create on ourselves, others, or society as a whole. Our primitive brain and its limbic system create our emotional distress and ineffective responses. There are no exceptions.

Backward Logic

While more traits of the primitive brain exist, a most powerful common thread runs through all of them—a sort of general disordered logic that I labeled earlier as backward logic. This part of our brain reasons backward, from outside in, and responds to life in ways that worsen any given situation.

Let's use a client of mine I'll call Mark as an example. One of Mark's ways of feeling worthy of love was to do everything himself. He believed that if he let someone help him, it meant he was weak. It turns out that all this doing it on his own left Mark feeling very overwhelmed and weak. Then his primitive brain's only response was that he must push himself more and try harder: *You wimp!* The backward logic concluded, *If others helped him, it means he was weak.* However, in truth, this logic led to feeling weak.

Here's a trademark of our primitive brain. The backward logic leads us to end up face-to-face with our darkest fears, feeling weak, being alone... Just fill in the blank with whatever you most want to *not* experience. Through reversed logic we come up with responses that create what we want to avoid. We're silent when talking would help, talk when silence would help, approach instead of backing off, and back off instead of approaching. You get the picture.

I like to think of this primitive-brain quality of trying to prevent what you absolutely *do not want* as being like those *Wanted* posters from the Old West. Imagine that instead, the lawmen posted *Not Wanted* signs. Each time someone saw the *Not Wanted* poster, well, the unwanted would be brought in to the sheriff. And, of course, the sheriff would say, "No, not *him.*"

Until we define and clarify what we do want, an action of our higher self, we end up with what primitive brain states we do not want. Fear searches for fear in order to prevent it, and then only finds fear.

One of the ways to offset this "not" tendency is through using intention. Much has been written about attention deficit, but I believe there also exists an intention deficit. By clearly setting our intentions in a positive way, we invite the universe to share the infinite generosity.

One other key belief of the primitive brain is that our inner world of thoughts and emotions is caused by our external world. Notice how easily this sets up a conflict between the self and others. Elizabeth provides a good example of this belief that the outside causes the inside. A woman in her fifties, she had developed a very close mother-daughter type of relationship with a girl named Cynthia, some years ago.

Elizabeth was in her forties when she took this teenage girl under her wing. Cynthia was considered artistically talented, but lacked any kind of nurturing figure. Elizabeth spent about ten years as a surrogate mother, nurturing and encouraging Cynthia, who began coming into her own and blooming.

Everything changed between Elizabeth and Cynthia when Cynthia met a man around her own age. He became her love-worthiness source, actually controlling and dominating her. No longer receiving encouragement to express her talents, Cynthia disconnected from herself and from Becky. Now, when Elizabeth sees a rather sad and emotionless Cynthia, she feels ignored, rejected, and hurt.

From our spiritual self and the place of One Truth, we can recognize that Cynthia had rejected herself in an effort to gain supposed love-worthiness—backward logic in action. Since she believed that this man held her love-worthiness, she would disown herself more and more, even though she never really got what she needed. Sadness naturally followed her loss of self.

Our personal truth, while not necessarily expressed, does not die. So, when Cynthia sees Elizabeth, she is reminded of her own rejected truth. Now Cynthia must reject Elizabeth at all costs to avoid seeing her own truth. Elizabeth had believed that she'd caused Cynthia to reject her, but this wasn't about her at all.

Actually, one part of this scene was about Elizabeth: Her backward logic set her up to believe she caused Cynthia to reject her. And in a subtle way, Elizabeth may have put Cynthia in the role of supplying her own sense of worth, based on Cynthia's progress.

However, once realizing the dynamics involved, Elizabeth could free herself from the hurt and judgment generated by her own place of deception. Elizabeth then restored the Sacred Sequence and remembered her own innate Truth.

The Law of Reflection

When we experience the One Truth, we know that events around us, whether conflicted or harmonious, result from our inner world. Notice how the relationships in your life actually *reflect* and maintain the beliefs you hold about yourself. The primitive brain implores you to convince others of your love-worthiness while surrounded by people who only reflect your own poor self-image. However, your truth resides within and presents opportunities for remembering your natural love-worthiness, the One Truth.

There is a subtle but important difference between your external life reflecting your inner world and what you *attract* into your external life. You've almost certainly heard of the Law of Attraction: This much-discussed law suggests that you attract into your life whatever you focus on with clear intention. However, there are exceptions. If you do not believe you are worthy, you will not attract the circumstance of your focus—no matter how clearly you focus with wonderful intention.

The Law of Reflection determines how much the Law of Attraction will work for you. These principles are long established in Eastern philosophical traditions. Your outer world reflects your inner one and the beliefs you hold about yourself. The universe will always unflinchingly tell you the truth; it never lies.

So, when the universe holds up a mirror to you, take stock and determine what needs to change *inside* of you, not outside. Use the Sacred Sequence to access the One Truth—faith, hope, love, and charity applied to God, self, others, and the universe—then find what you really believe about yourself from this perspective. The universe will mirror a much more appealing and accurate picture after you have found your One Truth again.

To summarize it in the simplest sense, our primitive brain takes over the running of our lives in response to emotional trauma. This fundamental error leads us to misunderstand ourselves, others, and life. We believe that some external, earthly source holds our love-worthiness; we must then somehow convince this source, or one like it, that we are worthy of love. But this strategy only leads to false deities, and various forms of compensations and addictions, with no satisfaction.

Each of us lacks some degree of awareness of the One Truth, God, and Divine Love. These areas are the parts of ourselves that experienced traumas. These traumatized parts long for love, but try to find it where it does not exist. In a sense, it might be said that all emotional issues are really about our awareness of and relationship with this Divine energy.

Our traumatized selves lost awareness of the One Truth, and has been mistaking humans for God and attributing human qualities to God ever since. We are then left confused and self-critical when our effort to rectify the misconception doesn't pay off. Our misconceptions about love-worthiness alter when we access the One Truth. Do know that the difference in our wellbeing is our awareness of this One Truth's eternal presence. Just because we forget doesn't mean it stops existing.

Before we move on to the next chapter and the particular types of backward logic, let's take a look at a list of the primitive brain's main qualities, and the place of One Truth. Each trait is really just a sort of energy that influences how we feel and function. Now try this with each of the qualities, starting with the first trait of the primitive brain, and then the first of the One Truth.

Step into the trait, try it on, and experience what you know as that trait. Notice how you feel inside yourself in terms of how your energy flows or feels constricted, how tight or loose you feel, and your emotional state. Each time we use primitive brain qualities, we impair and limit our true self. How much freer do you feel when trying on the One Truth qualities?

In review, the gist of the fundamental error can be seen by comparing the spiritual self with the primitive brain. The Spirit-self knows that love-worthiness precedes human life and endures beyond this life. This Truth residing within allows free access and expression of this Truth in your unique ways with nothing to lose: a life choosing from sufficiency.

The primitive brain believes that love-worthiness is missing and must be earned. Choices are made from a sense of deficiency. Personal action involves risk of failure to obtain worthiness, or endangers any portion of felt worthiness gained from external sources.

To clarify this for you, it may be helpful to list the general differences between our primitive brain and Spirit-self. Below is a short list of how each looks at self, life, and others.

Primitive Brain	Spirit-self
Type-A personality	Lives from spiritual self, Divine within
Believes life is a battle	Celebrates life as an opportunity
Judgmental	Accepts and appreciates uniqueness
Feels threatened	Looks for ways to uplift others
Microscopic perspective	Big-picture perspective
Analyzes	Experiences
Rigid	Flexible
Critical	Looks for solutions

Impulsive	Patient
Judges (crystallizes self-situation)	Observes (remains factual)
Concrete and literal	Abstract and symbolic
Blames others for life troubles	Takes responsibility for own choices
Exclusive	Inclusive
Acts in order to feel	Feels in order to act
Quick fix	Long-term solutions
Self-serving	Respects self and others
Do unto others before they do unto you	Sees God in all

CHAPTER 3

FORMS OF
BACKWARD LOGIC:
THE ILLUSION
MAKERS

As children, we display an amazing mixture of awareness as we adjust to living this human life. We still hold memories of our pre-birth relations with the Divine in the spiritual realm, but our limited neurological development limits us in early life.

The result is living day to day from just the primitive brain for about the first seven years of life. All the while, our spiritual purity randomly spills out in disarming clarity and wisdom. It's very interesting how we first learn to live as humans, then strive to reclaim and live our original spiritual nature.

The power of awareness is highlighted throughout this book. As stated earlier, awareness is the only moving part. No matter what we notice, events happen and the universe remains infinite and eternal; only our awareness alters. Our primitive brain operates with greatly restricted observational skills, which usually misleads us into inaccurate beliefs about self, others, and life.

In this chapter, we'll identify, explore, and learn how to expand beyond the restrictions of the primitive brain. Awareness of these reasoning styles helps us to break out of the constrictions, allowing us freedom of choice and ability to remember the One Truth.

Here we will explore the six types of specific backward logic and how they create the civil war within ourselves. Remember that we each use these reasoning styles; the difference is recognizing them, and shifting out of them to our spiritual self.

I will describe and give examples of each type of backward logic, and present alternative perspectives that can raise our consciousness to the spiritual realm, which allows a different perspective and solutions to former problems.

1. **Backward Logic:** The reasoning of the primitive brain, which believes everything outside of the self determines self-worth. It is also the cause of responding to problems by doing the opposite of what would be effective, only magnifying the problem.

2. **Egocentricity:** The perspective of the primitive brain, which believes everything observed is about the self or makes some statement about the self. This sets up a defensive relationship with life.

3. **Proximity:** Blinders on our observational abilities that limit us to just the immediate time and space of any situation. From this viewpoint, it is easy to form mistaken conclusions or beliefs.

4. **All or Nothing:** Seeing everything and everyone in terms of black or white, all or nothing, limits awareness and response options.

5. **Inductive Logic:** This primitive brain trait makes sweeping generalizations from single ideas or restricted amounts of information. This robs us of the uniqueness of life, limiting our awareness and choices.

6. **Transductive Logic:** The primitive-brain belief that two events occurring closely together in time form a cause and effect relationship, with the first event causing the second. This leads to mistaken beliefs about the self and self-worth. Guilt often stems from

this primitive-brain style.

7. **Irreversibility:** The primitive brain loses its memory about the quality of self and life before a trauma. This interferes with reclaiming the whole self and the One Truth.

The work of Swiss child development specialist Jean Piaget will serve here as the primary source for identifying the types of backward logic. Additional key contributors to research on children's thought processes include Robert Kegan and John Flavell, among many others.

Piaget studied the reasoning processes of children for several decades into the mid-1900s. He found certain trademark styles of reasoning that children use and are actually bound by, until they reach greater neurological development at around age seven. The result is that backward logic can only be used in early childhood.

Two powerful forces influence our self-concept and resulting sense that we are worthy of love: backward reasoning and our spiritual self. In the first instance, we are restricted to relying on the primitive brain for understanding life until around age seven. This unavoidable backward logic provides the necessary conditions for emotional trauma and all its future consequences.

The other influence—or opportunity, perhaps—is learning how to use our spiritual self as the rectifying and healing center for past wounds and adult life experiences. This process amounts to the Sacred Sequence applied within the self. Here we proceed through God, self, others, and the universe, with "others" being the traumatized part of the self. Furthermore, the universe here is the whole of the self, including how we treat our physical self.

The Sacred Sequence allows us to reconfigure our past traumatic memories. Think of it as repaving memory lane! Trauma is a response within us, not the external event. Events that happened in the past will not change, but the meaning we attach to them and how we feel about ourselves can and will change, when using the Sacred Sequence.

The illusion that haunts us from our past is not the event, but the meaning we believe it holds about us. No event or thing has inherent meaning. We assign meaning depending on what part of the self handles the assignment; we either suffer or thrive. Let's look at the types of backward logic and ways to overcome them.

Egocentricity: Why Is It Always About You?

Perhaps the key ingredient in all the styles of reversed logic is egocentricity, a way of looking at life that leads us to believe that the world revolves around us, that everything in life is about us. When we live from an egocentric position, we take to heart things that were never meant for us. The primitive brain takes everything in life personally, which ignites paranoia, self-protection, and conflicts. Egocentricity avoids responsibility for personal choices, blaming others or outside forces. In the process, we actually reduce our personal power.

You could think of egocentricity as the self-centered cousin of empathy. Empathy means we can put ourselves in another person's shoes. Egocentricity occurs when you place others in your shoes. The reasoning goes like this: *What I do is right for me, so it should be right for* everyone. That is the starting point of wars.

Everything that happens in life revolves around the self. Egocentric reasoning operates from the belief that events taking place outside of ourselves determine how we feel about ourselves. The drive is to control what occurs outside of the self. This reasoning is the epitome of the fundamental human error and loss of free will.

Egocentricity and its dynamics lead us to another sort of universal principle: That which we try to control enslaves us. Once we attempt to control some process, person, or situation outside of ourselves, we are required to dedicate our energies to controlling it. The result is that this person, process, or situation then dictates to us what, when, and how we must act.

We'll take a short trip here to observe this universal principle in action.

Let's visit with fictional David, who starts his own business. He begins his venture with great pride and excitement. David puts in long hours and achieves early success. He wants to control every aspect of his operation to ensure that everything is being done just right. David's business quickly reaches the point where he needs to add additional staff. Rather than seek competent, self-directed employees, David hires people who need his direction. Without even knowing it, he is setting himself up for frustration.

David uses a micro-management style and hovers over everyone. He finds they need his undivided attention and guidance. "Doesn't anyone know how to do anything around here?" he fumes. Soon his business starts to suffer as he shadows his employees, leaving little time to attend his own duties. David trusts his employees less and less, and even wonders if they somehow have it in for him. He works harder and harder, putting in more hours in the hope of fixing things. He has become enslaved by his employees.

Let's step back from the situation with David's business for a moment. Notice how our primitive brain gets us into such tight spots. If we believe this reasoning, then what goes on in the world around us determines our worth and competence. Egocentricity tells us that everything happening is all about us, and we fall for the distraction. We then try to fix the circumstances around us, instead of changing something within the self. Now we'll look at how our spiritual self knows another perspective.

Why Is It Never About You?

How do we get the self out of this egocentric position, and stop taking things personally? Here's a simple illustration: Take a trip to a store that sells house paint. Pick up one of those little paint samples, in any color you like. Then show this paint chip to ten or twenty people and ask their opinion about the color. The range of responses will vary from "Wow, that's beautiful!" to "Yuck; I hate that color." In this very simplistic experiment, our feelings about the feedback reveal our degree of egocentricity.

The absence of egocentricity, or reversing backward logic, allows us to recognize that the color shown to others is the same, no matter who looks at it. What *does* change is the person viewing it. This tells us that what other people express only reveals their inner world of perceptions, values, needs, and beliefs. Nothing anyone says or does is about us; we are not the color, nor did we create it. Just because we like the color and someone else does not makes no statement about our color taste or overall competence.

Now apply this truth to any negative belief you hold about yourself.

Who asked you to hold this negative belief about yourself? What egocentric motive led them to ask this of you? What did their request of you tell you about their perceptions, values, needs, and beliefs? As you identify the source of this negative belief, go into detail about the other people's perceptions, values, needs, and beliefs. By identifying details, you can begin to shed this negative belief, because you know it is not about you.

You can begin to see how other people could have generated this negative belief about themselves. You can notice how their words and actions were all about *them*, not about you. This loosens the formerly traumatic interaction with them.

Eventually, the details will lead you to find that the other people's words and actions were really *all* about them. In mild-to-moderate traumas, this realization can help to demagnetize the negative belief and allow it to eventually fall away completely. If you know that other people's actions are not about you, then you can let them go. But we must delve into these beliefs, not simply try to push them away.

Of equal importance is replacing the negative belief about spiritual truth and the self. The One Truth tells us that our very being consists of a pre-existing, permanent, unconditional love. This love precedes our conception and life on this earth, and surely existed before we ever encountered those who revealed their own negative inner world. Now sense and experience your immunizing original truth, and the difference this makes. This is the One Truth.

Proximity: So Near, and Yet So Far

Proximity is another form of backward logic that centers on space and time. How we interact with space and time determines whether we confine or free ourselves. When our primitive brain relies on proximity, we tend to use a small excerpt of time and space as the sole source for determining meaning in a situation. Proximity is like blinders, restricting our awareness of space and time.

We ignore the past and the future, confining ourselves to a small box. We don't look at how the ingredients got in the box. While there really is no such thing as the past, future, or time, we can learn how to approach and incorporate these concepts into more effective living.

Very often what happens at any given moment in time is more about the preceding time than the immediate moment. Everything that comes before an event contributes to whatever we express. However, the last straw can look like the only straw.

Proximity leads to us believe that the immediate moment caused the event. Couple this belief with egocentricity, and you come to believe that *you* caused the other person's behavior in that moment, or that the other person determined your behavior. This belief combination is common within the abuse victim syndrome.

The other prominent feature of proximity has to do with space. Proximity attempts to make sense of an event by using only the immediate environment surrounding the event. It may be that we only observe part of a room, part of a building, or part of the setting where the event takes place. We select a small part of the entirety of space and sever it from the meaningful whole. This general process is classic in the primitive brain. Segregated or dissected parts of a whole are used to create meaning, and then applied to the self and the unknown whole.

Our primitive brain works on the plane of earth where time exists, yet time operates as a contrived device best used for coordinating and organizing. Time does not exist in the world of the Divine, because all exists now. The hourglass, with its sand slipping through the narrow opening, becomes imposed on an otherwise eternal flow. The past exists simply as a figment of our primitive brain. Yes, the events did take place, but we are mistaken to believe in such a thing known as the past.

The primitive brain strings together these limited excerpts of time and uses egocentricity to determine meaning about the self. The truth is that these past events have no connection. The primitive brain is determined to link them together, forcing them into false meaning. Yet we live out this belief, making it self-fulfilling and perpetuating the illusion.

By noticing a larger space, such as the rest of a room, building, or setting, we can expand our awareness to notice benign or even positive space that restores context and changes the meaning of a space.

If Mary was eating dinner with her family when her violence-prone father erupted at the table, the space where they sat may become emotionally charged and distressing.

When Mary scans the larger space of the dining room and the rest of the house, what other events does she remember? Perhaps she begins recalling positive, loving memories with other family members in the same or larger space. This alters memories and meanings.

Our primitive brain also thinks of space as existing on the earthly plane. This earthly concept of space has limits, and items that only occupy this earthly space. In the spiritual realm, the one our spirit knows, there is only infinite space—no limits, no barriers. Once again, all is now.

One of the essential ingredients of emotional distress happens when using proximity. Our primitive brain forgets about the time that led up to an event: minutes, hours, days, months, even years. It also forgets about the role of the future, since words and actions are often motivated by someone's belief or need about the future.

Backward logic makes us forget about any space that exists outside the immediate surroundings where the emotionally distressing event happens. The result is that we may hold only a small visual memory of the time when we felt someone attacked our love-worthiness in some way. Our world shrinks, and it feels like this attack is all that exists in the whole world.

We literally and figuratively lose sight of other times, other places, and our true spiritual being when using proximity. There are ways to shift out of our primitive brain and reclaim our spiritual self; we can invite awareness of what is outside this tunnel vision time capsule by asking ourselves a series of questions.

Below is a list of these questions to assist you in gaining more awareness, and in the process, free yourself from limiting beliefs. As you try out each question, first take stock of your awareness regarding a person or situation. Observe how you feel emotionally, and how your body experiences the emotions. As you apply each question, notice how you expand your picture. What happens with your awareness and emotions, and how does your body experience this natural stretching?

So Far So Good

Some of the questions helpful for expanding out of proximity are about the person who we feel offended us. For example:

- What different kinds of experiences have you had over time with this person?
- What different experiences have you had in the same space where the offense took place?
- What positive experiences have you had over your lifetime?
- What different places and spaces have you been in during your life where you had positive experiences?

Notice how you feel as you stretch your awareness. What happens to your perspective about yourself as a result? What different view does this allow you of the former offense and offender in that old time and space?

Expanding our time and space consciousness allows us to remember the infinite picture. We leave behind the experience of constricted space and time, and the diminished love-worthiness that resulted. We begin to realize that there is always more to our being than any moment in time or any part of the infinite space. We exist as boundless love energy, transcending space and time. Holding this awareness and ability, we know and live our Divine connection.

All or Nothing: The Limits of Extremes

Black-and-white thinking comes with being a child; the gray areas remain invisible. As a game, children pick a flower and pull off the petals one at a time. With each petal plucked, they recite, "She loves me; she loves me not." Insert the gender of your choice here.

At this young age, a child never plucks a petal and says things such as, "She likes me as a friend," "Something may develop over time," or "We can just be bike-riding buddies." Any possibilities between the extremes of all or nothing are literally unthinkable to the primitive brain, by which we all live until around age seven. Rigid thinking holds the all-or-nothing perspective together, preventing flexible problem solving.

Notice how the extremes of primitive brain thinking may limit our choices regardless of age. Backward logic only provides a perspective in all-or-nothing choices when truly, just about all of life exists in degrees. All-or-nothing perspectives prevent negotiating or compromising, thus restricting possible solutions. It may also be true that a great deal of our frustrations in life stem from us forgetting that we possess freedom of choice.

We actually become angry about how our life feels constricted because of all-or-nothing thinking. Our primitive brain blames the external circumstance. The real source of our frustration usually remains on our inside. We feel angry about our perceptual limitations, not *what* we perceive but *how* we perceive. This backward reasoning has us feeling trapped.

The Constriction of Categories

Life begs us to place our experiences into categories. Maybe it is just so we can keep up with the incredible number of events and stimuli directed at us each day. If we left everything we experience in one category, it might be overwhelming. In some ways, when it comes to making memories, our brain is similar to a cabinet with countless files. Each folder has a heading, and we put our memories within whatever category we feel is the best fit. The problem comes in when we let our primitive brain do the categorizing.

Once we decide on the meaning of a situation, we then place this memory into the file containing what we believe are similar experiences. But how do we really know what any event in life means? Do we use our past to determine what the present means, possibly perpetuating personal myths? On the other hand, do we find that we can use our future goals to determine the meaning of our present? The latter lets us choose any event and turn it into a stepping-stone toward our goals.

As an example, Dana applies to the college she's dreamed of attending since she was twelve years old. However, she is turned down. Her primitive brain, with its all-or-nothing outlook, tells her that she will *never* attend the right college, and that will forever limit her professional success. Her primitive brain tells her that she should settle for mediocrity in her career, or pick a different career path. The constriction of categories due to all-or-nothing perception leads Dana to sense that her career is headed for a dead end, and emotional distress follows.

If Dana's spiritual self is activated, she can see this disappointment of rejection by her chosen college as just a turn in the road. She can apply to different schools and continue pursuing her career goals. Faith, hope, love, and charity allow Dana to trust that this change in plans may not actually be a loss. Her sense of love-worthiness remains.

Maybe this is just the natural arrangement of her life, or anyone's life. Primitive brain uses linear thinking, which means when life starts curving, the primitive brain judges this as a bad event. Dana can actually embrace this situation and believe it will lead her in the best of ways. By opening ourselves to possibilities while holding faith, hope, love, and charity, we nullify distress toward the self, the college of first choice, and life itself. The One Truth remains as our frame of reference.

Nothing Is Not Everything

What was the last movie you watched? What messages did it contain for you? How many different emotions did you experience during the movie?

It can be interesting when we talk with friends after watching a movie together. We may compare notes and ask, "What did you get out of that movie?" After discussing this with four or five friends, we start to realize how different people find different meanings. We may even ask, "Did you watch the same movie that I did?"

It is interesting how we can derive so many different meanings from the same movie, or from anything we observe. Has the same movie ever meant something different to you when you watched it again a few months or years later? What about a favorite book you read the second time? And how about music repeated time after time?

By now you get it: the same experience can mean anything, and any experience can mean everything. The result is that all or nothing becomes nothing is not all.

Choose your meaning and choose your life. Everyone and everything you notice is already embodying everything; it's just waiting for you to notice. We get to see what William Blake saw in the grain of sand.

Inductive Logic: Generally Specific

The following is not a riddle. Do you know the difference between inductive and deductive reasoning? The detective in a murder mystery identifies the killer by using deductive reasoning. A large pool of information and suspects is gradually reduced until the detective reaches a conclusion.

Inductive is the opposite sort of reasoning. In a murder mystery, you start with a suspect and then build a case to convict this suspect. Some would call this being framed. Inductive reasoning in everyday life is also called generalizing. We take a single example in life and decide it's true for every similar situation, everywhere, for all time. Pessimism is an example of generalizing in action.

To use an example, six-year-old Becky feels rejected by a friend at school. Becky then generalizes, and believes that nobody likes her anymore. As children, we can only generalize; we lack the cognitive development for more sophisticated thinking. Our primitive brain can only use inductive logic, or generalizing. This leads us to many misunderstandings, prejudices, and emotional distress. However, this generalizing way to frame an experience becomes activated in the midst of emotional trauma, regardless of age.

Bottoms Up

One of the ways that generalizing maintains emotional distress is when we generalize from an emotionally traumatic event. We become prejudiced toward people similar to the offender. For example, this could take the form of fearing people in positions of authority. Likewise, we may generalize about our love-worthiness, believing that others feel the same way about us as the original offender.

The result of this process can be that we come to believe our love-worthiness is determined by others. How we can persuade them to give us back our love-worthiness, if it is even possible? Emotional trauma sets in motion the classic and pervasive form of generalizing. We will explore more the dynamics of emotional trauma in another chapter, and invoking the Sacred Sequence to access the One Truth.

The more we generalize, the more we limit ourselves. Generalizing could be called bottom-up reasoning. We take a specific event and apply it more and more in a general sense to all of life. We may use backward logic to determine that our environment of people and things is somehow dangerous, and holds power over us. This belief is based on some encounter or series of encounters in which a person, not God, determined our love-worthiness. We then generalize this belief and apply it to other people and situations.

Top Down and Cruising

How is generalizing a form of backward logic? Generalizing robs each moment of its uniqueness. No two seconds are alike. I just claimed that nothing is not everything, making all into one whole. Everything does stem from the same infinite source, revealing the commonality at some level. However, the way each second and each experience manifests is a unique expression of the eternal infinite. We end up noticing how everything is simultaneously unique, yet of the same Source.

The opposite of generalizing reverses the backward reasoning. Instead of bottom-up reasoning, we use a top-down approach. This allows us to see the differences between each second, event, and person, thus freeing us from prejudice. We might refer to this opposite of generalizing as "unique-izing." Noticing the differences in life helps us dismiss the negative myths about our love-worthiness.

All-or-nothing thinking, proximity, and egocentricity can no longer hold us when we stop generalizing. Looking for and finding the uniqueness in each situation opens us to opportunities. Instead of walls, we find pathways. Finding uniqueness creates a map that gets us out of the confusing maze. We suddenly become aware of many alternatives and choices when all is new and different. We gain full and free expression of our spiritual self.

Transductive Logic: The Cause of the Effect

A different type of reasoning is called transductive logic. You know about inductive logic, which involves going from a specific point to a general point. And you know about deductive logic, which involves going from a general point to a specific point. *Trans-* means across, so transductive logic is reasoning that uses information across time and links it together, mistaking it for cause and effect..

The primitive brain is a logical machine; like all machines, it lacks flexibility and adaptability. The style of the conscious mind is to force any given set of ingredients to fit into its style of processing. Rather than observing what the ingredients add up to, the primitive brain subjects the ingredients to a limited style of processing, which limits the meaning available for any set of ingredients.

Perhaps the initial flaw is segregating ingredients into sets in the first place. These sets are then separated from the whole of infinity, misleading us into personal limitations.

Transductive logic is a close cousin of proximity; they tend to work together. Where proximity makes sense of situations by roping off a short period of time or a small space, transductive logic goes a step further. This logic forces a supposed common thread through the ingredients, across any given period of time and space. Thus, we work from a belief of the primitive brain that says when two or more events happen closely together in time, the first event caused the second one.

Here's an example of this logic. Several years ago, there was a television commercial for orange juice that featured two young children, about five years old, sitting on the front steps of a house. Each child held a small carton of orange juice with a straw extending out of it.

The scene took place in the early morning, just as the sun was rising. As the little boy started sipping on his orange juice with the little girl watching him, the sun began to rise. As he sipped more and more orange juice, the sun fully rose in the sky, shining more brightly with each sip.

In the commercial, the little girl looked at the boy, observed the sun as it rose, and then looked back at the boy. "Wow!" she exclaimed. Commercial message aside, the girl's transductive logic led her to believe that the boy caused the sun to rise by sipping on his orange juice!

Two or more events that happen closely together in time are believed to be cause and effect in transductive logic.

On a more powerful, life-altering scale, this logic of the primitive brain contributes to some children's beliefs that they cause their parents' divorce, or other turmoil in the home. Furthermore, children often believe they should fix, and be *able* to fix, the turmoil.

Let's look at an example that illustrates this process. Jennifer's parents announce their divorce two days after she brings home a poor report card. Now Jennifer believes that if she made better grades, her parents would have stayed together. From this point on, Jennifer may fight with guilt and sadness that stems from her perceived role in her parents' decision.

Jennifer may respond to this distress in one of two general ways. The all-or-nothing strategy of the primitive brain shows in forms of the extremes: She may become a straight-A student and hyper-responsible adult to "make up" for her supposed crime. However, she tends to enter relationships with people who are irresponsible. The result is that she feels she must always carry the weight, or the relationship will fall apart. The pattern will repeat itself, and the opportunity to invoke the Sacred Sequence remains rich until a shift happens.

Another response to the transductive logic may lead Jennifer to think, *What's the use?* She then puts little effort into school and her adult life, since she believes she's "bad" for causing her parents to divorce. The classic mantra of *I'm not good enough* may be heard here. Her self-worth suffers and she mistreats herself, dismissing her personal gifts.

This halfhearted effort in life and its poor results only reinforce her belief that she's no good. Since relationships with others reflect our beliefs about ourselves, Jennifer naturally chooses relationships in which she is treated badly. Until she goes inside herself and addresses her flawed logic and beliefs, she will continue putting herself in emotionally—and possibly physically—harmful situations.

How do we overcome transductive logic and reverse this self-limiting process? The first step is to revisit the ingredients we used in our original process of flawed logic. We first disassemble the belief system, separating the ingredients to remove any meaning we have assigned. This may not be as easy as it seems.

It is often difficult for us to recognize that near-simultaneous events can happen without linking them together in some way. Furthermore, this scenario of feeling responsible for a distressing event is not limited to something as simple as a bad report card. An irresponsible parent or many other circumstances can lead to a hyper-responsible child who recruits irresponsible relationships around her, or a person who abandons his or her own gifts and gravitates to destructive relationships.

While all aspects of life are in some way interconnected, it may not be in such a direct cause-effect way as the surface view suggests. The Law of Reflection reminds us that what we notice outside of the self reflects our inner beliefs, not necessarily any external truth. Yet the external circumstances will *seem* like truth, when they really mirror internal convictions.

Now let's revisit the scene of the supposed transgression, in which Jennifer brings home a bad report card and her parents announce their impending divorce two days later. On the human plane, it is helpful to identify other factors that may have contributed to each major event. The purpose is to expand awareness beyond the tight time and space (specific event) constriction imposed by transductive logic.

This expansion allows us to identify mental, emotional, physical, and spiritual elements within Jennifer that may have played a role in her school performance. What is going on, or not going on, within Jennifer that contributed to her bad grades? Did she naturally sense the tension and conflict in the home, which in turn disrupted her concentration in school? Does she simply need some tutoring in subjects that are tough for her?

This same sort of exploration and questioning also clarifies understanding of the factors that contributed to Jennifer's parents divorcing. What other mental, emotional, physical, and spiritual factors may have contributed to people in the adult relationship deciding to end their marriage?

There is another type of transductive logic we need to consider. The first one discussed refers to events that do happen, and the cause-and-effect meaning we give them. The other type of transductive logic involves what does *not* happen. This accidentally self-inflicted distress starts with "If only (some particular circumstance had come to be), I'd be happy (successful, rich, famous...)" You get it. We imagine that if some wanted event had happened (cause), then life would have turned out perfectly (effect). We ignore any other potential challenges or adversity that could happen in life, transporting ourselves to our version of Sunnybrook Farm.

This illogic holds an unobtainable, idyllic life out in front of us, mocking us. The untruth here needs to be replaced with the One Truth, so that we can allow ourselves the rich experience of constant love-worthiness.

From the perspective of the Sacred Sequence, it is useful to understand each person's relationship with the Divine. The degree of felt separation from the Divine determines our life choices. We choose from a degree of deficiency of spiritual awareness, or sufficiency of spiritual awareness. This awareness determines the healthiness of our life choices. We can then recognize that each person who makes unhealthy choices is just reacting to a sense of disconnection from the Divine, and that these choices are not caused by another person's actions.

Irreversibility: You Can Go Home Again

Irreversibility is another feature of our primitive brain. Once a trauma happens, whether physical or emotional or both, our brain finds it difficult to remember much about what life was like before the trauma. We tend to forget how we looked at life, how we felt, and how we acted prior to that event.

On a simple level, when you feel angry toward a loved one, you seem to forget his or her positive actions in the past. You just know that right now, this loved one is a _____! [Fill in your favorite epithet or expression].

In more significant life events, all we know dates from the time of the trauma forward, not before it happened. We find it hard to recall and re-experience past pleasant events or emotions. At best, they seem like long-lost, elusive memories; at worst, we are as detached from them as if they had happened to someone else.

Let's revisit Jack from the previous chapter. If you remember, he was raised by a mother with longstanding symptoms of depression. She rarely displayed any mood other than sadness. Like any child, he wanted and needed his mother's love and approval. And, like any child, he naturally had endless energy, curiosity, and a desire to explore the new world.

At around age six, he became better able to expand his world. He started first grade, and ventured off further and further from his mother. He naturally returned to her and shared what he discovered, hoping for her love and approval.

His depressed mother responded to him with barely veiled sadness that Jack saw and sensed as her disapproval of him. After many such experiences, he gradually found that he sensed more love and approval from her if he stayed near her rather than venturing off.

Jack did not know it at the time, but he was shifting out of his natural zest for life, sacrificing himself to his mother for her love and approval. The memory of his zest and love for life began to fade. By the time he reached dating age, he surprisingly chose to date girls who displayed an underlying sadness. He doted on them, and continued to put off his own life interests and development.

Now, coming into adulthood, Jack has forgotten his original feeling of how interesting life is, and how much he wants to participate in it. Actually, he has forgotten what he enjoys, beyond some vague sense of how it used to feel. Jack's mother became his source, so he contorted himself for her supposed approval and love. He has come to experience depression about his own loss of self.

Backing Up to Go Forward

Jack's recovery of his original self involves re-connecting to his awareness as a child that the world is full of possibilities. This recovery and reconnecting comes in part by going back to a time when he did know joy, love, and a natural desire to express himself. He reclaims his nature from within.

He then separates his mother's role as his source for love and approval, using the Sacred Sequence to remember the One Truth. This allows him to reconnect to the pure love of the Divine. He gradually realizes that this reconnecting actually encourages him to access and express his God-given self. Once he has experienced the Sacred Sequence, Jack gains the unconditional love he craves.

Through experiencing and embracing this unconditional love from the Divine, Jack can then resolve the underlying anger and sadness that stemmed from his relationship with his mother. He gains the freedom to send his mother unconditional love, since he now experiences an ongoing, ever-present source: God. Now Jack can celebrate the experience of living more fully, and develop relationships with others based on positive self-expression.

Notice the natural restorative ways of the Sacred Sequence and the One Truth. It starts with God, proceeds to self, others, and then the universe. We become aware of and experience the love and freedom we crave.

Now that we have identified and explored the types of backward reasoning, you have probably also noticed how these forms of backward logic knit together to form a belief system. This belief system then dictates life choices, including how we treat ourselves.

Many, if not all, of our misconceptions start with an emotional trauma in a relationship during childhood. Our primitive brain processes the experience. Once the primitive brain processes the trauma, we then make this traumatizing person our all-powerful deity, living in homage to him or her. We use this human as our reference, making a generalization for how we think of God. The pressure is then on us to compensate for our supposed shortcomings, and rectify this feeling that we are not worthy of love..

This reasoning is very subtle, very general, and yet incredibly powerful. Subtle or general energy affects many things, while obvious or specific energy manifests as one thing. The whole process is a bit like sleight of hand: We often don't even notice it happening. We simply react to the illusions of the primitive brain, without questioning or knowing the basis for why we feel distress or disharmony. This self-deception is another aspect of the primitive brain, as it has no willingness to examine the self.

These reactions we live out come in the form of a mental and emotional reflex to compensate for the discomfort of the illusions that our reversed logic created. In the next chapter, we will identify and explore these compensations, and learn how they complicate life. In the process, we will also find how these illusions cease when we apply the Sacred Sequence to resume living the One Truth.

CHAPTER 4

COMPENSATING FOR THE ILLUSIONS: THE "-ICS"

We each try to deny the contusions of our illusions, but the "-ics" will not fix the tricks of the collusions. This may sound like something from Dr. Seuss, but we'll decode this truth as we progress through the chapter.

Here we will explore our common reactions to the illusions created by our reversed logic. Let's take a closer look at a concept that is somewhat playful, but substantial at the same time. No, this is not a description of a vintage wine—playful, yet substantial. This concept is what I call the "-ics."

When we compensate for our illusions, we develop an over-reliance, or even an addiction, to certain lifestyles, types of people, activities, status, or substances.

To break it down a bit, the term *alcoholic* is just the word *alcohol* with -ic added as the suffix. Yet we misuse the term frequently, calling a person who loves chocolate a chocoholic, for instance. Truly, the term for this chocolate-lover should be *chocolateic*. Just add -ic, and addiction is implied.

With this in mind, we will identify and explore the various -ics used to compensate for the emotionally painful illusions that we eventually treat as truth.

A certain principle runs through the compensating effort made by the primitive brain. It consistently relies on a particular belief. The notion that *If some is good, then more is better* serves as the credo for the primitive brain. This belief means that if the compensating choice works, even a little bit, then increasing the effort of this compensating is better.

Unfortunately, the primitive brain invokes the same credo even when the compensating strategy stops working. This strategy is somewhat like the all-or-nothing perspective of the primitive brain. Self-evaluation is not part of the egocentric brain, so it just continues at the effect of this belief.

The "Materialist-ic"

Since backward reasoning leads us to believe that what exists outside of the self is what counts, it becomes easy to measure our worth by the quantity and quality of our possessions. The addiction that follows may result in an endless loop of material acquisitions: buying, buying, and more buying. The purpose of the buying is to verify and reassure the self about love-worthiness.

The logic of the materialistic sounds something like this: "If I can acquire all these possessions, then I must be effective and competent and, therefore, love-worthy." Furthermore, "Everyone will see these fine possessions that I own and will recognize my worthiness." However, this strategy turns over the power to others, who must see and be in awe of the amazing possessions.

At a deeper, spiritual level, the materialist-ic is actually trying to buy God and the love that comes in relations with this being. Imagine that—God is the new chair or the new—car! In a way, it's true, since God is all the energy of the universe.

But what's at work here is the "materialist-ic" attempt to rearrange the Sacred Sequence into others, self, God, and the universe. And so, it continues: acquire possessions that others will notice and they will praise you; then you can feel good about yourself, and then maybe God will accept you for your accomplishments. On the other hand, as with each order sequence, it just creates an addictive relationship with possessions as the "fix."

Two basic scenarios seem to account for most of the motivation in the materialist-ic person. The first happens with the person who grows up in a family with few possessions and little money. Maybe peers taunt the person about their less-than-stylish clothing at school. Maybe the person compares himself or herself to others who appear to have more possessions and better things. Such individuals may then use reversed logic to conclude that they are inferior to others, and that the only way to make this right is to acquire more things.

This process results in comparing the self to others who have more, then acquiring more possessions. But there is always somebody who has still more. The belief is that these possessions can act as tokens that can then be cashed in for love-worthiness. Remembering that the One Truth precedes all actions can free a person from this cycle.

The second scenario of the materialist-ic happens when *things* are substituted for love. Some parents do not give love in the form of pure emotion; they give money or things as their show of affection. (The money is often exchanged for material things.) This can mislead the child into believing that such materials equal love. The more things they have, the more lovable and love-worthy they become.

Surely, the adult child can experience love-worthiness after purchasing a bigger boat or a bigger beach house. However, the nature of addictions and external sources for love-worthiness leads to only brief satisfaction before the individual feels compelled to make the next purchase, then the next, and another...

Addictions fool us into believing that we can satisfy them and put an end to addiction. But the truth is that this process of satisfying only sets us up for another round of addictive behaviors.

A crucial element of maintaining addictions of any sort is that we absolutely must ignore the negative consequences of the addictive behavior. If we actually acknowledged and focused on the negative consequences, how could we consciously repeat the same self-destructive choices?

Different, Yet the Same

This leads us to another universal principle. It is interesting to notice how the same behavior or expression of the self can stem from opposite roots. Emotional and financial deprivation in childhood can lead to an adult who compensates for it by acquiring countless possessions.

Likewise, consider that the child who grows up in a family that substitutes lots of money and possessions for love can also become an adult who acquires countless possessions. These nearly opposite roots can bring about nearly identical compensations. Different roots, yet the same form of expression occurs.

In addition, this common root issue with opposite forms of expression often brings two people together in long-term relationships. This couple ends up in serious fights about money, although they share a similar emotional wound and root issue. The common ground is where the healing can happen, not the opposite forms of compensating.

Now don't get me wrong, plenty of families have few possessions, little money, and children who do not become materialist-ics. Love is their currency, and it flows freely. This child learns that love is free and unconditional, and finds love-worthiness early in life. No compensations are necessary.

This universal principle has a second part to it. The same childhood experience of substituting money and possessions for love can result in the exact opposite manifestation. For every reversed-logic illusion, there are two general compensation styles. This is the more or less principle, which is a cousin to the all-or-nothing style of the primitive brain. The person still tries to gain full compensation for the illusion with possessions in the more style of compensation. In the second compensation style, less, the person *avoids* all possibilities of gaining material power or other compensation.

The avoider gives away personal power, becoming subservient or refusing opportunities to make money or develop a career. The avoider prevents loss of love-worthiness by never acquiring it. This is an example of backward logic designed to remedy backward logic. The gist of this principle is that the same experience of love deficiency likely results in one of two reactions: self-indulgence (more) or self-deprivation (less).

The "Power-ic"

One of the effects of emotional trauma during childhood involves doubts about our personal power. We encounter a conflict with a significant adult, and reversed reasoning leads us to believe that our personal power—our will to manifest, and ability to effectively deal with life challenges—is in danger of becoming extinct. The primitive brain logic tells us that other people will try to take away our power. We then create an illusion that says every situation and every person poses a threat to our personal power.

The power-ic cannot let others become emotionally close. Others can't be trusted, because they pose a threat to power. The power-ic may live by the mantra, "Keep your friends close and your enemies closer." The dynamics resemble the king or queen who believes they might be overthrown at any time.

The "power-ic" must keep others ignorant since knowledge is power. Have you ever worked with anyone like this before?

The power-ic comes to believe that the external environment—not the internal one—is the source of power. While the power-ic often rises to a position of authority or power, it is not necessarily because he or she is the most qualified. Power-ics feel compelled to find a way to be on top so that they feel power over others and the environment, in order to ease their own fears. This is rampant in our society.

However, this strategy only maintains the insecurity, since we're only as powerful as our last display of power. The addiction means we must use this external display of power repeatedly, because an external display is what the primitive brain requires. Notice how an absence of trusting others serves to reflect an absence of trusting the self. With self-trust, there is no need to verify personal power; one just knows and trusts in the infinite availability of Divine energy, and uses personal power in accordance with life purposes.

The "Man-ic" and "Woman-ic"

These -ics involve the role of relationships for some people. Our relationships with our parents and significant adults during our childhood creates lasting impressions, and influences our sense of love-worthiness. We form bonds and learn much about ourselves, others, and life, even if we develop some misconceptions along the way. For better or worse, these early relationships form a frame of reference, to which we compare all future relationships.

No one gets out of childhood unscathed. We each experience some form and extent of emotional trauma. What we do with these experiences—as well as our interpretations, their supposed meaning about the self, and how we respond—makes all the difference in how the trauma affects us.

An emotionally traumatic event happens in the physical world between two or more people. The traumatized one observes this physical world event and uses the primitive brain to make it about the self; distressing emotions follow, and conclusions about the self, others, and life result.

Adding to this detrimental process are the conclusions made about the relationship with God. The backward logic starts with others, then applies to the self, and then to God. The human trauma may lead to a sense of unworthiness to receive God's love, unless this black mark on the self can be removed. On the other hand, it is God's love that exposes the black mark as a human-made myth, removing it, and replacing it with pre-existing love from God.

Our sense of love-worthiness is never more evident than when we become involved in an emotionally intimate relationship. This emotional closeness exposes beliefs formed by reversed logic. We seem to preserve our deepest issues for our most intimate relationships, as we put our love-worthiness on the line in them. We find out just how much love-worthiness we possess when we engage in these emotionally vulnerable experiences.

The "woman-ic" is the man who goes from woman to woman in relationships. He may stay in a relationship for a few weeks to a few months, but remains ready and willing to move on to the next woman. He usually lines up the next relationship before leaving the current one. Sometimes this woman-ic finds satisfaction in the conquest. He reasons that if he can win over this woman, then he verifies his love-worthiness. Again, the primitive brain is almost never convinced, so it calls for another "victory."

The fix is fleeting, and the woman-ic needs to verify his worth again and again. The chemical high that comes from the early stages of a romantic relationship may serve as the cocktail party that provides relief from his fear of being unworthy of love. This process is not the same as sex addiction, which is another type of compensation. The woman-ic is addicted to women who will verify his worthiness. The sex addict is addicted to the act itself, and the excitement of the short-term sexual act.

The man-ic represents the female version of addiction to relationships with men. Shared roots exist for both versions: doubt about one's love-worthiness. The presence of a relationship represents and translates into the thought, *With (him or her) in my life, I must be worthy of love.* The silent rejoinder is, *Without (her or him) in my life, I am not love worthy.*

This closeness helps to offset the fear of abandonment or rejection that had been interpreted to mean one was not worthy of love. Keeping a relationship close at hand provides compensation for the primitive brain. Part of the solution is to go against the first reflex of indulging the fear. Allowing the primitive brain to express itself fully leads to understanding, then more easily leads to reconnecting to the One Truth.

The challenge for the man-ic or woman-ic is that the fear of abandonment is never addressed. An unresolved issue never goes away on its own; it is only dormant for a brief period after a fix. As a result, what had briefly provided relief soon becomes the source of insecurity. The very relationship that soothed the fear may soon result in the man-ic or woman-ic feeling very vulnerable. *What if (he or she) decides to leave me?*

The response to this fear leads to clinging for dear life, or leaving before being left—the more or less principle. The addicted one loses the self by sacrificing in order to keep this other person in his or her life. Such addictive people may search for replacements before the current relationship ends, and will soon jump ship to supposedly safer territory. The addiction cycle continues until the underlying fearful illusion is addressed and resolved.

There are variations to the compensating strategies of the man-ic and woman-ic. Another response to this doubt of love-worthiness is to avoid intimate relationships at all costs. Also, some people engage in an ongoing series of short-term relationships, ended at their choice or whim to prevent rejection. A self-deprivation reasoning strategy comes to life here: *If I don't get involved with someone, then I can't be abandoned or rejected.*

Staying in a toxic relationship is another variation. The toxic relationship is often based on disrespect or abuse. The relationship addicted person holds the belief that he or she must somehow convert the disrespectful or abusive person into a loving individual. Failure to do so only verifies the deep, dark fear of lacking love-worthiness. The process of transductive logic plays a role in holding this scenario together.

Notice how this process involves the addicted person placing his or her significant other in the role of god. The significant other holds the power of life, death, and confirming love-worthiness. The Sacred Sequence naturally restores order. The One Truth dissolves the addiction bond, freeing the person.

Abandonment in a relationship is translated with inductive logic to mean *I must not be worthy of love, if (he or she) left me.* External dictates internal in the world of the primitive brain's backward reasoning, meaning that what happens outside of the self determines what's believed on the inside.

A more accurate motto might be "What happens outside stays outside." Instead of dealing with abandonment that happens on the physical plane, recognizing the ever-present Divine love within ourselves shores us up to overcome the insecurities and doubts about our love-worthiness, leading to "What happens inside stays inside."

The "Food-ic"

The food-ic is also rampant in our society. Foods of various kinds and amounts can serve as compensation for different needs on several levels. This multilevel process of compensating makes dealing with food addiction especially challenging. Food can offset illusions about our love-worthiness and the associated symptoms of anxiety, depression, loneliness, boredom, fear, and anger. A former client of mine equated abundance of food with success in life. He relied on a pattern of overeating to confirm his success, and ultimately, his love-worthiness.

Many people eat simply to change their mental and emotional state. For every food we eat, our body's physiology responds in a certain way. These chemical reactions make food a drug to our brain and body. Comfort foods are described as such because they increase serotonin levels, which generate a temporary mood lift and calming effect. This comfort temporarily offsets the emotional distress created by illusions about our love-worthiness.

Power-ics, as described earlier, may find that a caffeine-infused energy drink is just the tonic to fuel their drive for power, offsetting their illusions. Foods high in sugar can provide a boost in energy and temporary relief from the doldrums of boredom or depression.

Perhaps a common thread in each food-ic is the presence and influence of stress. Ordinary, everyday life presents a certain amount of unavoidable stress. Stress might be defined as anything that we believe poses a threat to our safety, wellbeing, or love- worthiness. Stress is not about an event, but our *reaction* to an event. Stress is what happens inside—mentally, emotionally, and physically—in response to the perceived threat.

Life naturally presents situations that can easily result in a stress response. Whether it's a job interview, asking someone out on a date, your child's first date, asking for a raise, or buying a house, life presents uncertainty. Stress-free living is not realistic, but stress-managed lives are possible. Our primitive brain determines the difference between temporary, fleeting stress and ongoing, chronic stress.

Along with many others who teach mindfulness, Jon Cabot-Zin, an expert in the field of stress management, offers books and teachings that provide very helpful methods of stress relief. Mindfulness leads to perspectives that allow us to override the primitive brain and activate our more effective self.

Short of a genetic trait or some other physical condition, people often eat too many and too much of unhealthy foods in response to the stress. Emotions such as anxiety, worry, boredom, sadness, and anger easily lead the food-ic to accept food cravings when in search of a quick remedy for the felt emotional and chemical imbalance. Yes, some people do lose their appetite in response to stress, and just don't eat—the stress-eater's envy.

However, the deception of stress for the food-ic creates the belief that any given situation represents the *source* of stress and poor eating choices. Forgetting that we always have choices disempowers us. Awareness of choice provides a personal power that can set us free. Every revolution, whether social or personal, begins with awareness of choice.

I would suggest that the difference between chronic and temporary stress is our relationship with the Divine. Situational stress becomes chronic if our love-worthiness is already in question. Identifying the source of our stress response makes all the difference. The process of dealing with stress and bolstering our relations with the Divine is a bit like a leaky roof. The rain is not the problem; the hole in the roof is the problem.

Shoring up our uncertainty with the ever-present Divine love can override situational stress, providing a deeper reassurance about our love-worthiness. For the food-ic, food becomes the Divine rather than being the product of the Divine. If we fill up on the energy of the Divine first, we can then decide what and how much to eat from a place of sufficiency rather than making our choices from a place of deficiency.

The "Calm-ic" and "Calmphob-ic"

Many people grow up in homes filled with chaos and chaotic relationships. Whether the chaos stems from substance-abusing parents, physically abusive parents, or some other source of chaos, this atmosphere of unpredictable eruptions takes a toll. Unless otherwise disturbed, we naturally gravitate toward a state of calm.

However, when emotional eruptions repeatedly pierce the calm, this state of calm becomes scary. The calm before the inevitable storm results in a state scarier than the actual turmoil. Again, we end up with two general paths of reaction to this trauma. We generally either seek a state of calm at all costs, or *avoid* a state of calm at all costs.

The calm-ic is a person who has become addicted to the state of calm. This person sees calm as more important than just about everything else in life. Such individuals seek it and preserve it with great determination. Calm-ics may avoid situations that hold potential for turmoil. They may choose instead to live life from the sidelines rather than participating in life, avoiding stimulation, challenge, and change.

In contrast to the calm-ics, the "calmphob-ics" actually fear calm so much that they *seek* turmoil. They may feel it's better to work with a known enemy than risk the unknown time bomb called calm. When growing up, the longer the calm went on, the more frightening life became; they knew it was just a matter of time before the volcano erupted. When these people reach adulthood, they seek or purposely set off the volcano as a means of feeling more in control and less afraid.

With either strategy, there exists the belief that the power to determine the inner world resides in external situations. Moving toward a solution and resolution involves accessing the ever-present specific resources provided by God, so that they can hold these provisions as their source of security and calm.

Naturally, the condition of calm is not the problem. On the other hand, through conditioning and inevitable associations, we come to believe that calm is dangerous. The real truth is that holding on to the calm state within can act as a life raft in stormy seas. Our primitive brain has us jump overboard when the seas get rough.

This Source of calm can be held, or we can be held by this Source, as we weather life's inevitable storms. This Divine Source never wavers, granting a consistent state so that we can adjust our self-concept, relationships, life, and relations with the Divine accordingly. Calm is not determined by another person; calm happens between ourselves and God.

The Alcoholic and the Drug Addict

The most classic -ics are the alcoholic and the drug addict. Substance abuse and eventual addiction are motivated when these substances alter the user's mental or emotional state. The goal of the addict is to shift out of an unpleasant state and into a more desirable state, or to experience oblivion to forget the emotional pain.

Eventually, a chemical or brain addiction occurs. However, the original need for shifting states actually starts from an emotional trauma that misled these individuals into a negative belief about the self. This other human who traumatized them served as their disapproving deity.

The irony of the primitive brain is that its strategies for solutions are so shortsighted that they actually contribute to a more substantial problem over the long run. Look around your life, city, country, and the world for countless examples of how the primitive brain perpetuates problems.

The substance-abusing person usually holds a sense of shame at a deep emotional level. The self-concept suffers from severe negative human judgment. Yet what does this person usually feel, after abusing some substance (self-abuse is really what happens) to avoid experiencing shame? Shame! The principle here is that when using reversed logic to resolve an emotional issue, the result will be an experience of the unwanted emotion! Reversed logic places us in an inescapable loop of frustration.

How will the rejected person ever feel worthy of love? The Sacred Sequence became inverted by the primitive brain, going from others to self to God. Now love-worthiness is derived from a fickle human, instead of an unwavering God. We then use backward reasoning to conclude that God must also be fickle, and that our faith, hope, love, and charity are only as good our last act of perfection—so we compensate for the lost love that we "caused."

The solution to the common -ic is simply the inverse of the inverse. *Huh?* Yes, restoring the Sacred Sequence is the solution that brings us back to the One Truth. Our primitive brain is generally horizontally *and* vertically dyslexic.

We start the backward reasoning by deciding that someone outside of us determines our inner love-worthiness—the horizontal dyslexia. Next, this limited brain puts this someone else in the god role. We place a human before God and decide God must be like this person, whether he or she is kind or cruel. This is the vertical dyslexia.

Inverting the inversion leads us to connect and commune with God by experiencing faith, hope, love, and charity. Faith opens the door to love. Only by experiencing this faith and the infinite loving generosity of God can we come to know the One Truth: pure love precedes our existence, and simply *is* our very being. Through knowing and feeling this love as the essential ingredient of our existence, we can experience the eternal fullness from within. Upon realizing that this love is secure, we can stop chasing it and/or compensating for its previously felt loss. Be still and know.

The Common Cure

Each of these -ics starts with a common process of reversed logic. In addition, each of them resolves with a common solution. The process that leads to our emotional wound and pain leaves out the crucial ingredient of God and the available love-worthiness. We use illogic to assemble a self-concept and sense of our love-worthiness in a virtual vacuum, using only our earthbound experience because the primitive brain doesn't sense anything beyond the tangible.

This vacuum deprives us of unconditional self-love and God's love, which would resolve our emotional distress and satisfy our spiritual longing. Even though we may move forward in life in many fine ways, with much self-development, our emotional wound remains deprived of healing until we reconnect this aspect of the self with the Divine.

The wound cure starts with restoring the Sacred Sequence. We then bring this God awareness to the negative beliefs we hold about ourselves. What supposed aspect of the self was considered bad, and what negative beliefs did we form about ourselves?

Bringing the God awareness to this aspect of the self, we then observe the self from this sacred perspective. This faith, hope, love, and charity toward God, then self, and eventually others brings a new awareness that untangles and absolves old wounds. We'll delve further into these wounds and solutions in the final chapters.

In this chapter, we identified our general responses to the illusions created by our primitive brain's backward reasoning. The purpose is to stop reacting on autopilot, and call into question the foundation of these compensations so that we may rise above our primitive brain to restore the Sacred Sequence.

There are many different forms of compensating, certainly more than those presented here. How do you know if you are compensating for an illusion and suffering from the -ics? Usually, when we compensate for some emotional wound, we overindulge in something or deprive ourselves of something. This something may be relationships, fun, money, material possessions, food, and power, setting emotional atmospheres or various mind-altering substances.

It can be a bit tricky to differentiate between compensating and a healthy lifestyle. One way to know the difference is by looking at how these choices affect your life. Take honest stock of how your choices influence your physical, emotional, mental, and spiritual wellbeing. How do your choices influence your relationships, career, health, and finances? No denial allowed here. In the last chapter, you can find and use these discoveries to address and reconcile your own -ics.

In the next chapter, we'll explore our emotional experiences. What is the nature of emotions, and what purpose do they serve? Our emotions form a set of bookends that serve as a catalyst to action and an endpoint or result of action. Our primitive brain can easily become a helpless slave to emotion, always seeking to avoid discomfort and find comfort.

However, there is more to our emotions that just seeing them as aversive or pleasant. Emotions are not solid, rigid forms to be taken literally, as our primitive brain would have us believe. This universe is fluid, which allows us to move, shift, and choose instead of being at the mercy of what comes our way. We can make of it what we will.

Emotions carry messages about our perspective. Learning to interpret the message of emotions empowers us. The next chapter delves into the world of our emotions, where we can learn to understand and translate them, finding that they provide powerful opportunities to remember the One Truth.

CHAPTER 5

EMOTIONS AS PATHWAYS TO WHOLENESS

We rarely experience anything in life without also experiencing some sort of emotion. As Francis Bacon put it several hundred years ago, "Experience without emotion is void of learning."

So, what we can glean from this is that the emotions we experience in life teach us something. This something that we learn depends on the state of mind we use to interpret the events and emotions. Most importantly, we learn how to use our states of consciousness.

Let's begin by looking at the general nature of emotions, along with how the primitive brain and Spirit-self bring emotions into our lives. We will also explore the effect of emotional trauma more closely. Then we'll consider how emotions provide opportunities to find pathways back to wholeness.

Rather than falling for how the primitive brain misunderstands emotions, we'll learn how to interpret the messages of emotions from a higher, broader perspective. The chapter finishes with an exercise for you to use, reclaiming parts of the self that feel lost due to trauma.

Different people experience different emotions about the same event. As individuals, we may even experience a variety of mixed emotions about a single event. Some people develop such skill at meditating or mindfulness that they may reach that place of awareness separate from emotion. However, most of us usually experience life with some type and degree of emotion.

What are emotions? Where do they come from? What function and role do they fill in our lives? I won't pretend to provide complete answers to these questions—and certainly not in a single chapter—but we will find some solutions that can empower each of us to find the benefit of any emotion. We can also develop some ability to embrace and alter the energy of emotions.

It seems that emotions result from the particular perspective we take when thinking about an event. Not that this is news, but emotions result from our point of view. However, the important thing here is that the primitive brain *doesn't know this*. This primitive, egocentric self believes that if it experiences some emotion, then it must be true. The primitive brain views the universe as static or stationary. Furthermore, since the primitive brain lacks self-awareness, it can't examine its own perspective or see others' points of view.

This lack of self-awareness and flexibility locks the primitive brain into a reactive mode. The life-changing difference is that our Spirit-self doesn't take emotions personally, or as unchangeable "facts." Our spirit knows that the universe is an ever-changing, fluid system. This means that emotions provide feedback about our perspective. When we shift perspectives, allowing ourselves to rise above the primitive brain and review events, emotions change and free us. Emotions might be loosely categorized as pleasant and unpleasant; the pleasant ones we enjoy experiencing rely on love as their foundation.

I suggest that unpleasant or uncomfortable emotions exist in just three fundamental forms. Anger, sadness, and anxiety seem to represent the basic unpleasant emotions. Numerous cousins such as frustration, hopelessness, or worry exist as variations of these three basic unpleasant emotions.

Jealousy, for example, is an interesting mix of all three of the base emotions—anger at someone who's receiving recognition-approval when we're not, sadness about losing needed recognition, and anxiety about what this event means about our future needs being met.

The whole collection of emotions appears dormant, each existing in some sort of suspended animation. Once we take on a certain perspective about something, the emotion activates and we experience the energy of this emotion. It also seems true that once we experience an emotion, we then tend to see everything through this emotion.

As mentioned earlier, nothing in this life comes with inherent meaning. We each decide what something means to us. (The philosopher Jean-Paul Sartre comes to mind.) The difference in this process of assigning meaning comes from the part of self we use to interpret an event or an emotion: our primitive brain or our spiritual-self.

Trauma is not an event; it's a response that calls for treatment, just as stress represents a response and not an event. Once an emotional trauma occurs, our trauma response takes over and wants to be in charge of deciding the meaning in our lives. The challenge with this is that the primitive brain uses those illusion makers of the previous chapter, and views self, others, life, and God though this lens.

Now the primitive brain believes that another trauma will occur. It looks for anything that resembles the past circumstances of the trauma, and reacts as if the feared event is recurring. The primitive brain trusts no one, including the self, and feels compelled to somehow get this black mark—a trauma that negates love-worthiness—erased.

Now let's look at some other factors that influence our emotions.

The Four Ingredients of Being and Doing

Once again there are four significant pieces to this puzzle of how we move through life; free will, perception, beliefs, and awareness.

> **Free will** is what we put into action, or non-action. The subtle form of will reveals itself when we allow. Allowing is one of the most powerful abilities we possess. We'll explore this further in Chapter 7, on faith, hope, love, and charity.

Perception is what we observe with our senses and then interpret. We give meaning to what we observe. For example, I am wearing a blue shirt. What happened to you in the past when you or others were wearing a blue shirt greatly determines what a blue shirt means to you.

Beliefs represent a conclusion, so to speak, about what we observe related to the self, others, or life. Notice that beliefs automatically include and exclude elements.

Awareness—is the scope of what we consider time and space—how broad and how high or deep. Our awareness is the only moving part in all of this, and contributes the most influence to our life experiences.

The four ingredients awareness, beliefs, perception, and free will strongly influence our thoughts, emotions, behaviors, needs, and values. Our awareness is the only moving part. It determines how we use our free will and what we believe, since we can only use what we perceive from any amount of awareness.

If the color green is all I am aware of in the color spectrum, then this is all I know and use. We now know that infrared and ultraviolet exist. What else exists that we do not yet know?

Our level of awareness sets a framework from which we perceive, make meaning, experience emotions, and then respond. Beliefs tend to determine perceptions—meaning that we suspend our beliefs and just use working hypotheses, with no emotional attachment needed. Optimism and pessimism represent beliefs that determine the meaning of events in our life.

Beliefs are almost always limiting in some ways. Beliefs limit us because they include and exclude; the difference occurs when we experience something instead of just believing it. We live at the mercy of our willingness to suspend our beliefs.

Every emotion already exists, as though it is on some sort of cosmic menu. Our perceptions or point of view determine the meaning of an event, thus activating our emotions. By changing perception or perspective, emotions naturally change, which then activates different interpretations and response options.

The meaning of any event in life is greatly determined by how we believe this event will affect us.

Have you ever said something like, "If Philip doesn't call soon, I'm really going to get pissed off!" Well, Philip doesn't call and the anger-fest starts. This predetermined belief sets us up to experience anger unnecessarily. We decided through egocentricity that if Philip doesn't call, then our life—our worth—is somehow damaged. We gave Philip our personal power, then got all pissed off at the poor guy who doesn't even know he's become our emotional master.

When we look back at an event that led to anger, we often find a spot along the way where we made a decision to deny our own truth. The truth about our anger is that we feel angry about a decision *we* made to give away our power. We let go of our free will—actually gave it away, and allowed someone else to direct us. Here is the harmful version of the power of allowing.

The supposed culprit—the other person—is no longer the source of the problem. We can return back inside ourselves, recognizing the opportunity to reclaim the self and our personal power by choice.

We can find our personal power again by tracing our emotions back to our thoughts, then to our beliefs and perceptions. What we're really angry about is our perception. Yes, Philip to some extent, but the real power is in our perceptions—not Philip.

What is this process called perception? Perhaps the real trick or skill to perceiving is how not to let our past determine the meaning of our present or future. Our primitive brain tends to superimpose our past on our present. This is really just an imposition!

Once trauma happens, the primitive brain decides that in order to feel safe, it must scan for anything in the environment that resembles the environment in which the trauma took place. This scan includes people, places, things, time, and even colors, sensations or smells.

An especially unfortunate aspect to this primitive-brain search for safety is that it believes that if nothing in the environment is dangerous, it is just a matter of time until danger appears. It becomes clear just how much trauma deprives a person of living in the moment with the opportunities for true safety and fulfillment. When safety is the only concern, we detect only that which is related to safety.

Reversing the focus of the primitive brain's hyper-vigilance would lead to its scanning for ways to verify safety rather than danger. This method reveals a very different environment and feel. The environment becomes disempowered while the self is empowered. Self-reassurance happens here, along with reliance on the inner self for security. Notice the inner trust developing from this style, since it is often sorely lacking in those with significant traumas.

The odd paradox here is that those with little self-trust tend to live with a kind of naïvety toward others, often blindly trusting only to get hurt again. The lack of inner connection to their own trust deprives them of their sensor to know if another person is trustworthy.

How do we get out of the trauma response and into our more effective spiritual self?

The first step is to recognize that emotions are messengers, providing us with feedback about our perceptions. Emotions reveal how we're observing an event, and are not the only way of perceiving it. Once we step back and consider how we're seeing something, we can regain the ability to choose and shift our point of view. This shift gets us back in touch with our awareness.

Now here's an interesting way to consider emotions: These feeling responses may generally reveal either an old unresolved emotional wound or emotional freedom. What? Yes; if old wounds exist around some past event, then an established emotional reflex exists. If there is no old established emotional response, you're emotionally free.

For example, if while watching a movie you see and hear the father yelling at his son, maybe you feel sick to your stomach, angry, and sad, and have a flashback to your own past. This response provides a pathway to resolving this old wound. If you did not experience a similar situation of your dad yelling at you, then watching the movie won't evoke emotions out of proportion to the movie scene.

Our emotions inform us as to what we need to resolve. Remember, unpleasant emotions reveal an unmet emotional need. We can use this information to address the need rather than let the primitive brain tell us we should not feel this way. The primitive brain wants to reject the part of us, which already experienced rejection from some significant other in our life.

Another crucial step in effectively shifting out of trauma response and into our more effective self involves expanding our awareness. Once we interrupt the emotional reflex, we can then step out of i, allowing us access to our awareness level.

To illustrate this point, imagine walking in the woods. Stop anywhere along your path and just take a look around—all the way around. Now take a step further and look around again, and one more step, and... You get the picture. Each step provides a point of view with its own version of truth, and each is different. Each view is part of the whole, but no single view *is* the whole. Making meaning, forming beliefs, and the emotions that result only tell us about a small piece of the whole.

A primitive-brain point of view would use the one spot in the woods and determine beliefs and meanings for the whole forest and all forests, then take the resulting emotions as the only truth. Furthermore, even if the primitive brain took another step into the forest, this new view would now be the only view. The primitive brain lacks the ability to retain perspectives from the past, which limits the ability to integrate parts into a whole.

The spiritual self would utilize varying spots in the woods and remain aware that even these are just samples of the whole. Our points of view, the meanings we make, and our beliefs remain open for adjustment. Emotions, while always true, represent just a point of view—not the only or full perspective.

This way of looking at circumstances does not mean that we don't point out injustices or negotiate change in situations or relationships. What it does mean is that we examine our perceptions *first*. Once we gain flexibility in our perceptions, we can look at circumstances from different points of view. We are then more able to effectively negotiate change in ourselves and our lives.

Understanding Emotions

Unpleasant emotions tend to be rather sticky and hard to let go. Deeply imbedded within them and keeping them activated is an unmet need, which until identified and resolved within the self, is bound to stick around.

In contrast, pleasant emotions slip away more easily, like a helium balloon rising up and away upon release. These pleasant emotions are void of need, so they just float around for you to freely access and experience.

You must choose to hold pleasant emotions in order to continue experiencing them. And you must choose to let go of unpleasant ones for change to happen. Use your free will here. The primitive brain believes there must be a reason to feel any particular emotion. Your Spirit-self knows you can choose emotions and utilize these as helpful resources in shaping yourself and your life.

The most important aspect in all this is that we can learn to expand our awareness and then activate different emotions and responses from a higher part of the self. In general, we just reverse the process of how emotions come to life. We'll go through an exercise later in this chapter that will guide you to different consciousness and emotions.

Rather than progressing from perception to belief and meaning that leads to emotions, we start with our emotion and go backward to access our perception. We ask the self to remember just how many points of view exist. We come to better recognize that we can choose a perspective knowing that facts do not change, but the meaning of these facts vary according to our perspective. Now we regain freedom and our spiritual self.

Recalling the various types of reversed logic of our primitive brain, these styles of illogic invite unpleasant emotions into our awareness. Sure, we can illogic our way into pleasant emotions, building up our egos, but these "positives" are as misleading as the negative (negative = negating self-worth). If we label and judge experiences in life, then the emotions result from backward reasoning.

Now we experience the self-generated consequences and become our own threat. When we live by our primitive brain, we sever our awareness of the constant Divine Presence. It turns out that our perception is the problem, not the event. This perspective excludes those times when something or someone truly endangers us, such as when the lion is out of its cage at the zoo. The primitive brain will save you here by getting you to safety.

Truly, any situation already represents the whole, the all of the universe. It's just waiting for you to notice this ultimate whole. Once you do, you free yourself and find choices.

A Book by Its Cover

The primitive brain believes that if we feel a certain emotion, then this emotion is true. Your Spirit-self knows that emotions act as messengers, informing us about our perspective and level of awareness. While each perspective contains its own truth in that view, the difference is not taking emotions literally, or as an unchangeable truth. Rather, we recognize emotions as pathways to healing old wounds.

As I sit in this room, I can only see three walls. To my primitive brain, then, this room only has three walls. If my primitive brain turns around 180 degrees, it sees three walls again. So, yep, this room only has three walls. There is no carryover from one view to the next.

If the primitive brain does not see or detect something, then it does not exist. But the amazing paradox here is that if there *may* be danger around, the primitive brain does not need to detect it. Just the possibility of danger leads to believing something dangerous is here now or will be here.

Wow! How do we get past this imposing belief system? Our reflexive brain has a hard time recognizing fluidity, or any quality other than a static state. The primitive brain believes that if we acknowledge how we really feel about someone, the self, others, or some situation, we'll become stuck with or held captive by this emotion.

Well, as usual, the reflexive brain got it backward. By not acknowledging how we really feel, we *are* held captive by this emotion. Emotions won't change unless we acknowledge them, in the first step of the change process.

Welcoming the Unwelcome

The first step in finding a different perspective is to actually welcome the unpleasant emotion that exists because of an unmet need. Now, this unmet need may just be for expanding awareness, shifting perspectives, and then reconnecting to the Sacred Sequence and the One Truth. At a simpler level, the need may be for validating the self and reclaiming self-confidence, self-respect or reassurance about a relationship's security. Yet each of these "simpler" needs really just leads us to the need to remember and experience the One Truth.

Welcoming the unpleasant emotion goes against the grain of the primitive brain, which is how we know it is helpful. It reverses backward reasoning, providing the solution. According to developmental psychologist Robert Kegan, the first stage of personal change is emotional discomfort. I would add that the first stage of change is resistance.

If we resist unpleasant emotions, we actually supply more energy for the unpleasant emotion. It becomes stronger through our pushing against it. How tiring and distressing it is, to constantly try to push away anxiety! We start feeling anxious about feeling anxious, accidentally creating a double layer of anxiety. This resistance may be the definition of suffering, at least from an Eastern philosophy point of view.

The biggest opportunity imbedded within the unpleasant emotions you experience is that they provide an open door to your past wounds. Rather than rejecting the unpleasant emotion, connecting and understanding the perspective begins the healing process. By understanding these uncomfortable emotions, you can follow the path back to its point of origin, an emotional trauma from your past.

Let's use an example of a man who was raised by a very stern father. During his childhood, James was criticized by his father at every turn. Whenever James would attempt to do something, his father would only notice what he had done wrong or missed. These criticisms, received when James was expressing himself through a task, carried the impact of an emotional trauma.

James rarely, if ever, received compliments or "good job" comments. As a result, James lacked confidence in himself and his abilities. The old familiar "not good enough" chorus sang loudly. James actually said, "My father took all my confidence."

This sense that someone, an offender, took something from us—self-confidence, calm, trust, etc.—reveals the sort of energetic disconnect that happens during trauma.

Now graduated from college and in his new job, James carries forward his childhood experiences—generalizing, as the primitive brain does, and expecting his new boss to criticize him. James will receive criticism of his work, but he will interpret the criticism as personal, since the primitive brain manages egocentricity. Since he expects this criticism, James finds that he holds back in expressing himself and is tentative in work decisions and productivity. His self-suppressing is the problem, not his work per se.

James's *reaction* to his trauma-driven expectations brings—sure enough—criticisms from his boss about effectiveness and productivity at work! Now James gets the verification he expected and further generalizes, "Man, the whole world is against me." This same belief spills over into James's personal life. He expects others to find him unacceptable. But it isn't the whole world; it's the fractured self that prevents James from using his wholeness.

The primitive brain makes a deity of the trauma source, or the offender, believing it holds his salvation. But more importantly, our continued existence or extinction is determined by the trauma source, endowing it with the qualities of a most primitive god—threatening, vengeful, fear-based, and bullying, with "comply-or-else" threats. How we separate from and rise above this misconception generated by the primitive brain and learn to live from our spirit represents the core essence of this book.

While a full collection of ways to reclaim the self and remember the One Truth can be found in the last chapter, here is one way to reclaim the lost parts of ourselves: We're returning to the scene of the trauma. We seem to shed certain personal qualities in the midst of a trauma, losing part of the self.

This lost part of the self may also contribute to the obsessive tendencies we experience around a trauma. We may know at some level that a part of the self is missing. We just can't quite put our finger on it, so we just go back in our mind to the last time we possessed this quality.

The first step in reclaiming the lost quality is to name it. Identifying the quality or trait helps us gain a specific connection to this part. It also helps us to recognize it when we find it.

In the case of James, self-confidence is a reasonable name for the lost quality. When you think about self-confidence, what sort of image or color comes to mind to represent this energy or state of mind known as self-confidence?

These symbols used by the brain to represent events and emotions may be colors or icons that mirror a myriad of perspectives and emotions. These icons may be thought of as similar to symbols found in dreams. Do not let your literal, primitive brain interfere with this exercise.

For James, the color green comes to his mind. The shade of green matters here as well. Emerald is the color James sees when he uses his mind to give him an icon for self-confidence. Feel and experience the energy of this.

The next step in reclaiming is to go back in time to find the emerald green. Just drift back in time to the places of trauma, finding the one that seems like the earliest available. Search the scene of the crime like a detective until you see the emerald green. You will. Just open yourself and search with emerald green in mind, and it will show itself.

Upon seeing the green, let yourself reclaim it in any way you like that allows you to take it within yourself. Sense the energy and how it feels in your body and your awareness. Notice the difference with self-confidence.

Your inner skeptic may be saying *this seems absurd*, but it doesn't understand. Just open and allow yourself to find what you know. Once this green and the energy of self-confidence is in you, move forward in time and notice the new perspectives. Come to the present, then look into your future through this newly reclaimed self-confidence.

The differences in perspective with self-confidence include such things as gaining separation of the self from your work. You are not your work, yet you find you can more fully express the self in work and away from work.

Just notice the dynamics of self-confidence. A stronger connection to the self brings you into contact with the Sacred Sequence. Notice how the confidence leads to faith, hope, love, and charity. These stepping-stones then bring you back to the One Truth.

The primitive brain believes that external forces determine and control these valuables, so we feel vulnerable and at-risk. Knowing what's missing means that we recognize these intangibles exist *inside* ourselves from our inception, and cannot be taken or lost other than through misperception or constricted awareness. We are granted these qualities through the infinite generosity of the Divine. These valuable assets are not in short or limited supply; they exist in unlimited supply, as eternal energy of the universe accessible through our own awareness.

Continuing with these fear-based emotions, recognize that each of them stems from some sort of feared loss. Anxiety and worry result from anticipating a loss, while sadness results from believing we have already lost this aspect of life or the self. The death of a loved one is an exception to the roots of sadness, but it can slip into loss of the self. (This actual loss is another matter and has nothing to do with anticipation.) Recovering to whatever extent possible involves different challenges to expanding our awareness, and recovering the self.

To go a bit further into understanding the message of anxiety and worry, notice how the only way we can experience anxiety is to leave the facts of the present and make up various future outcomes. But there are no facts in our future! It is actually impossible to generate anxiety when we remain in the factual present.

We are okay now, and only become anxious when we make sentences with the word *if* in them. *If* opens us to the infinite possibilities but, when our primitive brain runs the if show, it becomes a scary movie. We find bad situations and dead ends, disempowering ourselves.

When our higher self or spiritual self runs the if show, we find desirable, empowering possibilities and options. Adding in the Sacred Sequence, we supercharge this awareness with faith, hope, love, and charity toward God, self, others, and the universe. Anxiety just needed to remember this larger presence.

The message of anxiety is feedback to remind us about the Sacred Sequence. Anxiety, as well as anger and sadness, are nothing more than by-products of perspectives that lead to forgetting. Remembering the Sacred Sequence releases unpleasant emotions, replacing them with reassuring comfort.

To recap, emotions provide us feedback, not literal information as the primitive brain would tell us. Every emotion already exists, in either active or dormant form, just as all energy already exists. Our perspective on any situation activates emotions associated with the particular perspective. The broader and higher the awareness, the more our perspective activates pleasant emotions. We become more resourceful with greater awareness, allowing us to access the Sacred Sequence and the One Truth.

Emotional trauma challenges the self, because trauma activates the primitive brain. The perspective of the primitive brain activates forms of anger, fear, and sadness, inflaming the effects of trauma. Certain "preventative" actions driven by the primitive brain are taken, along with primitive-brain beliefs and perceptions forming. These reactions bring unwanted additional trauma by creating behavioral-emotional loops of repetitive events and outcomes.

Emotional trauma results in a sense of loss, as a trait or traits of the self are dropped during the trauma event as a means of surviving. Reclaiming these traits involves identifying the particular traits, and receiving a mental image of these traits and their energy. This identity and quality of the trait is then used to travel back to the scene of the trauma to find and reclaim the trait. This trait is then integrated back into the self for use now and in the future, through envisioning the future.

In some sense, the very act of reclaiming and integrating a lost trait reconnects us to higher realms of being. We access a more open, broader awareness and perspective in order to do the reclaiming. The reclaimed trait restores our more complete self, allowing us to reconnect with the Sacred Sequence and then to remember the One Truth.

CHAPTER 6

REACHING NEUTRAL

It is not always necessary to access your highest consciousness in order to feel well and function effectively. In this chapter, we're going to identify several ways to step out of the traps of the primitive brain so that you can regain your neutrality and freedom of choice. Below is a list of the methods by which you can reach a place of comfortable neutrality.

- The big three
- The freedom of ambiguity
- The beauty of clarity
- Needful perceptions
- Closed loops
- Portals to the Divine
- The bubble of is
- Nothing to compare
- Peripheral vision; the not to untangle the knot
- Ego-withdrawal symptoms: "I make nothing I use"

The Big Three: Patience, Foresight, and Flexibility

When looking at issues we call problems and our associated emotions and behaviors, we find three essential missing ingredients: patience, foresight, and flexibility. These qualities not only provide tools for us to manage life better, they also offer us a way out of our survival mode perspective, since they are the opposite of the survival mode traits. Also, since these three traits travel together as a group, accessing any one activates all three and brings them into awareness.

To alter an approach to a situation in which you feel uncomfortable, first notice the primitive brain traits of impulsiveness, shortsightedness, and rigidity. Now shift and notice the larger picture that comes with patience. Pausing provides a larger view, which then naturally allows foresight and flexibility, awareness of possibilities, and options.

Sense the subtle energy of each of these three traits within yourself. Try out each of the big three, and notice what you experience within and how you feel

Finding the Point of Diminishing Return for These Three Qualities

It's important to realize that each of these three qualities can be taken too far and lose their benefits if the primitive brain commandeers them. Consider patience as purposeful waiting, not passivity. Flexibility serves well as change with a goal in mind, not necessarily abandoning the goal. Foresight allows awareness of potential consequences of choices, not overwhelm with possibilities. Use your choices as the template to evaluate possible outcomes, instead of just looking at the freestanding infinite possibilities by themselves.

The Freedom of Ambiguity

This skill bestows the ability to tolerate the unknown, suspending fear and beliefs to access faith, hope, love, and charity. The big three also come into play, as patience provides the ability to pause without prejudice. This pause allows the fog to lift, revealing truths.

The Beauty of Clarity

We may not always like what clarity brings at first, but notice how clarity also brings simplicity. It allows you to use your abilities and skills to better direct yourself toward satisfaction (satisfaction = satisfying action). Clarity exposes truth, and isn't this what we truly want? The truth does set you free, even if at first you may not like the truth you find.

Hope can serve as a bridge, supporting you through the transition of a new choice. With clarity, you come to know an accurate picture and can choose more easily. Notice how clarity and ambiguity work together, even though they first appear to be opposites. If you can tolerate ambiguity, you are rewarded with clarity.

Needful Perceptions

If we *need* circumstances to unfold or proceed in a certain way, it interferes with taking stock of how things really are. Here we see the two-sided coin of ambiguity and clarity. Needful perceptions prevent us from tolerating ambiguity. If I am driven by a fear of being alone, then I need to believe that this new relationship will meet my need. I will blind myself to truth, trapping myself within my illusion-driven need.

What is making this personal need so strong, and what are we not noticing at a higher or deeper level that can assist with this need from the *inside*, not the outside? This need provides another point of entry into old traumas and fears. This belief about ending up alone comes from forgetting the One Truth. Fear of ending up alone often comes from past broken trust and discomfort about receiving.

This personal need for a situation to be a certain way uses the primitive brain's qualities, or deficits, to interfere with the otherwise natural flow of the universal energy. The Sacred Sequence can provide an internal safety here, replacing the external insecurity. What do we notice, and more importantly, what *escapes* our notice when we perceive from a place of need?

Need leads to attachment to outcome, and this prevents our greatest good from being served. The situation becomes frustrating. We may be tempted by our primitive brain's perspective to say "damn it," but what the primitive brain does to the Divine Flow is dam it.

Closed Loops

We may not always consider the goal behind our actions toward others. There seems to be two primary drives: the response of the other person (external), or our integrity (internal). Where we place the emphasis makes all the difference.

As an example, remember a time when you walked into a store and the door was not an automatic one, but required you to open it. You noticed someone walking up behind you, so you held the door open for him or her. The other person caught the door and then entered the store behind you without uttering a word. How did you feel?

An open loop asks the other person to respond in a certain way. Notice the set-up for irritation, both for yourself and the other person. A closed loop only involves your inner standards and your behavior. If your behavior matches your standard, then you succeed—no response is required from another person. This closed loop allows you to remain in a neutral or positive position.

Portals to the Divine

Within every facet of life, there exists a rhythm. This rhythm can be found in nature as well as biological or choice patterns, such as doing or buying things. The cycle may be short or long, slow or fast. Just pick a cycle or a rhythm and tune in to notice up-down and on-off of the pattern flowing. Now focus on the part between, which happens just after the overt action. This between, a sort of pause, provides a beautiful portal to the Divine through the action void.

If the overt action is primitive-brain driven, meaning it has an addictive quality like one of the -ics, then the gap may initially lead to some form of sadness, anxiety, or anger. Allow yourself to sit with this and tolerate it, drifting down through the layers until reaching the void—a nothingness that grants access to pure Truth.

There exists an opening, whether between breaths, notes of music, a leaf touching down, buying something, or finishing a task. (For a meditation program useful for this, see Wayne Dyer's book, *Getting in the Gap*, published by Hay House, December 1, 2002.) Notice the subtle energy here as well as the opening, tracing it all the way to God. Notice just how many portals exist in life and this feeling! Fill the portals with your awareness and enjoy!

The Bubble of Is

Many years ago, there was a movie about a boy who lived in a bubble. This unfortunate boy had no immune system, so he was at risk for catching any and every virus out there in his environment. If he did catch any of these viruses, he would not be able to recover, since he had no immune system. The potential result could be out-of-control illness and eventual death. To provide some protection, this boy's caring parents devised a clear bubble of suitable material with an air filter system for this boy to live in safely.

But there does exist another sort of bubble in this world, one that is invisible and yet protective in a different way. Negative thoughts, stress-producing perceptions, and the resulting emotions are all a bit like a virus. These harmful thoughts, perceptions, and emotions can wreak havoc within us, sapping our energy and leaving us depleted. We can even catch them from others.

You know how it is; you spend time around someone who puts off this negative energy and the next thing you know, you've started your own negativity farm.

Meanwhile, your energy level goes down and you start perceiving life through negative lenses. Now, somehow you have to rid yourself of this uncomfortable negativity. The simple and almost reflexive urge is to go in search of some food—the bad stuff, you know. You allow the food to act as the "pill," to offset the emotional discomfort.

The instinctive choices for this prescription include the high-carb, high-fat, and high-sugar foods that hurt you with delayed side effects of increased weight and harmful physiological strain. Turning to mindfulness, and the live in the moment mentality provides a solution, and more importantly, provides a distress prevention component.

Truly living in the moment—the present—makes it impossible to generate anxiety, which is always about what the present *may* become in the future. The primitive brain uses words like *could* and *if* that take us out of the present and into the future, which contains no facts. Within the bubble of is, you connect with the Holy and the One Truth, recognizing its eternal and constant presence.

The process of mindfulness provides a protective bubble by living in the moment. Numerous books, workshops, and retreats teach the principles and practice of mindfulness. Living in the now is the foundation of mindfulness. You could think of a moment as consisting of just the facts in this moment, the is of the present: what is true and factual *now*. You observe the factual truth of the moment without analysis or judgment. As you reside within the is of the present, you encircle yourself with a protective bubble that keeps out the past and future. You form a protective bubble of is.

Inside the is, you just observe the present without comparing it to the past and without speculating about the future. Not that you don't see your past or envision a desirable future, you just utilize the present to direct yourself toward your desired future. Your decisions in your present determine your future anyway. Use now to make then.

This bubble of is provides a place free of the detrimental perceptions, thoughts, and emotions that happen when we analyze, judge, or compare. While this place of safety and comfort exists, recognize that you will step out of this bubble from time to time; we all do.

There are too many temptations to not step out of the bubble and wonder about the past, or speculate about the future meaning of the present. Just watch the news. What percentage of the broadcast is factual news, and how much is pure speculation? How tempting it is to follow in these mindless footsteps!

Notice how this speculation generates a sort of pull, tugging at you to step out of the bubble of is. Maybe you're just thinking on your own about the past or the future—wondering, comparing, or judging. All of these actions, including judgment, require us to invoke the future and/or the past, and step out of is and into what if. This opens us to the infinite, since all things could be. Once in the infinite, it will consume you—it never ends! How overwhelming and exhausting.

Remaining within the bubble of is provides what we desire emotionally, mentally, physically, and spiritually. This position provides immunity to the potential emotional distress of the past and future. During our time within the bubble, we observe what is and make no judgments, comparisons, or speculations.

Once establishing what is present in your own awareness, you can then begin moving forward, not just observing but interacting and utilizing the facts of the moment.

You simply work with the facts of the moment, which is all you really have access to in the first place. Using only the available moment minimizes frustration and maximizes a sense of freedom and control. Mindfulness does away with the need to compensate for distress, since the bubble of is prevents stress and distress.

Interestingly, there exists an odd paradox about stepping out of the bubble of is. While just being within the is, you experience comfort, safety, and peacefulness. It is impossible to generate anxiety, depression, or anger while being only in the present. Notice that these emotions require you to make comparisons in the present or go into the past or future. Comparisons naturally invoke the past or future.

The Attention-Deficit Disorder quality within each of us sometimes leads us to stray from the protective is. In fact, we often experience an *intention* deficit! Intending to remain in the is bubble is to experience the safety and peacefulness. Once we leave the bubble, we fall prey to all sorts of distress, then we make efforts to offset it. But none of these coping attempts really solve the problem, since we stay outside the bubble while coping. Once we leave the bubble, the only thing we really want is to feel what we experienced in the bubble. So why leave?

The brain seems to operate from a self-serving perspective of fear and self-protection. It seems very difficult, even mind-boggling, to flourish peacefully. There appears almost an innate disbelief about receiving abundance in life—not necessarily money and material goods, as the brain easily pursues these—but an abundance of wellbeing and loving experiences.

Can our primitive, inner self learn to receive and relate to this kind of abundance? The biggest hurdle seems to exist with regard to wondering if we deserve it. Yet, by the very constant offering provided by Source, we find our deservedness already mute.

During Nelson Mandela's inaugural address, he shared a quote written by Marianne Williamson. These words beautifully describe the dilemma that we each face in life:

> "Our deepest fear is not that we are inadequate. Our deepest fear is that we are powerful beyond measure. It is our light, not our darkness that most frightens us. We ask ourselves, Who am I to be brilliant, gorgeous, talented, fabulous? Actually, who are you *not* to be? You are a child of God. Your playing small does not serve the world. There is nothing enlightened about shrinking so that other people won't feel insecure around you. We were born to manifest the glory of God that is in us. It's not just in some of us; it's in everyone. And as we let our own light shine, we unconsciously give to other people permission to do the same. As we are liberated from our own fear, our presence automatically liberates others."

We tend to fear our own power and crave it at the same time. How much energy do people spend trying to undo or offset others' power for their self to feel safe, rather than just using their own positive power to feel safe? We often rely on external means of verifying our power, like influencing and attempting to control others or events.

Instead of an external reliance, consider acknowledging your own inner power and its constant presence. No one else can access your power; no one can diminish or take away your power but you. You may accidentally give it away or deny your own power, but only *you* can do this. Only you possess and choose how to use your power.

No Judgment

Once we judge someone or something, we become blind and deaf to any information that differs from our preconception. We deprive ourselves of truths. At some deep level, we recognize this disconnect from the truth—both the truth here on Earth, and the One Truth. This loss of Truth becomes the problem.

We realize this subconsciously, and distress begins. However, our conscious mind has no clue as to why we experience distress. The primitive brain feels convinced that the source of this resides outside of the self—the illusions—but as always, the Source resides inside the self.

Judgment results in the very thing it criticizes: ineffective choices. The process crystallizes anything it observes, thus freezing it into ineffectiveness. The result impacts self. So, the lack of effective action that receives criticism may turn into a sort of self-paralysis. The restricted awareness that produces judgment simply restricts the one criticizing, while everyone else moves freely. Free yourself!

Nothing to Compare

Comparison requires unnatural observation—taking excerpts out of an otherwise infinite eternal flow, either within your own life, or between your life and another's. What disconnection from the One Truth leads to the need for a comparison, and how will additional disconnections, stemming from comparisons, restore the connection?

To resolve the dilemma, replace the time and space excerpts back into context, sending excerpts into the All, leaving out nothing and thus leaving nothing to compare. Again, notice how the All awareness brings a natural alignment and renders any other questions moot. All that exists, once the excerpt is replaced into the whole, is the inseparable All. This All—whole—is the place of no questions. Nothing need be asked here, since only Truth resides.

False Negatives

Maybe you've heard of false positives and false negatives; lab tests sometimes yield inaccurate results. A false positive happens when the test result incorrectly indicates the presence of something significant. The false negative means the test falsely indicates the absence of something significant. All right, enough lab schooling.

We're going to apply these concepts to beliefs about the self so that when we believe something positive about ourselves that is overinflated, it might be called a false positive. You know the type of person who displays a big ego; this is a false positive in terms of his or her overinflated beliefs about the self. Furthermore, it's ironic, because this overinflated view of the self stems from the "successful" compensations the individual made in response to *not* feeling love-worthy!

The false negative refers to the accumulated negative beliefs about the self. Why call them negative? Because these beliefs *negate* self-worth. Each limiting, harmful belief about the self stems from trauma and the part of our brain activated in response. This part knows how to get us out of harm's way, but has no clue about what led to the traumatic event or what it means. This bully of a boss oversteps its authority.

It's like lying to cover up a lie; we just move further and further away from the truth. There is only one thing that will correct this multilayered process: the Truth. Moving back into Divine Truth is simply a one-step process. In the case of the One Truth, there is no use in arguing with these false negatives.

The part of our brain that produced these limiting, harmful beliefs is immune to any reasoning other than the fear-based kind. This part of our brain will not get it, and will not give up its position—no matter how strong the argument. Just go, and you will know that allowing what you want excludes what you do not want!

For day-to-day management of this self-critical brain, consider these two strategies. In response to a self-critical remark, follow it with three to five things you have done well. This change of focus shifts the part of our brain in use, and it takes a few repetitions to stay in the new perspective.

The other strategy is that if self-criticism is offered, then it must be followed with at least one idea for a constructive solution. This also shifts the part of our brain in use. Well, okay—here's a third one. Do you notice how the criticism is about the self, and not the choice? The criticism is off the mark from the start. Make any criticism just about the external (the behavior), not the internal (self).

Moving back into the One Truth provides the point of awareness that quiets all the arguing. Do not try to get the false to move into the positive; rather, move your awareness into the positive to apply this Truth, re-perceiving and remembering.

Peripheral Vision: The Not to Untangle the Knot

Our eyes possess two ways of observing. We have foveal vision, which focuses directly on an object. This foveal vision increases our energy and brings us into readiness for action. Foveal vision is a kind of tunnel vision, excluding objects outside the narrow focus. Sound familiar? This type of vision is used most often by our primitive brain, and excludes much information.

The other way our eyes notice objects is through peripheral vision. Think of it as a wide-angle lens that allows you to stretch out your visual field, noticing objects indirectly but in larger amounts. Peripheral vision uses no focus and thus shifts our energy level, allowing us to relax.

You will also notice how peripheral vision allows you to experience a blank mind. Since there is no focus with the physical eyes, there is no focus with the mind's eye, either. No science—just experience this and notice the calm mind and your body's response to this free floating. This absence of focus provides an interesting point of access to the Divine. Simply hold the peripheral vision—the not focus that untangles the primitive brain knots—and allow yourself to experience the Truth of being.

Ego Withdrawal Symptoms

What to do with all this space, time, and energy since all is now?! Consider experiencing the state of simply being. This effortless, natural state allows you to receive, experience, feel, and know at a higher and deeper level.

CHAPTER 7

THE SACRED SEQUENCE

This chapter is only for your heart. No brains allowed, and please, no clichés when it comes to the meaning of faith, hope, love, and charity. The words in this chapter will help you discover and experience your own versions of the energy that is faith, hope, love, and charity from Divine relations. You may find different, additional awareness as you experience these words. Whatever you discover, the goal is to leave behind brain-devised dogma and connect to heart-centered Spirit.

What It Is Not

Just to clarify, using the Sacred Sequence does not create the presence of the Divine in our life. The Divine is already and always present in us and in our life. However, we each experience pockets of limited or lost God awareness in various aspects of ourselves and lives. It is in these areas of trauma-induced limited awareness of God that we experience distress.

What happens through utilizing the Sacred Sequence is that we remember our original awareness of the ever-present Divine throughout our whole being. This awareness of Spirit then restores our ability to live effectively through the Infinite Source. Through living the Sacred Sequence, we can gain access to our own unique relations with God. No need to chase, persuade, or earn the abundance of this loving Spirit. Instead of generating ideas, actions, and life, we receive.

Imagine yourself as a solar panel, just receiving and then applying this energy where you choose. This constant and permanent connection brings security and peace from within, knowing that our Source resides within our very beings. These four elements—faith, hope, love and, charity—act like wires that plug us into the four levels—God, self, others, and the universe—bringing them to life.

What It Is

The Sacred Sequence reminds us of what comes first; not the earthly illusions about self, life, and others, but our pure spirit as an extension of the Divine. This earthly life consists mostly of illusions, since it is tangible and temporary. The real life is the intangible, invisible, and immeasurable that remains forever. Bringing this immeasurable eternal presence into this life creates an exquisite union.

Why is the Sacred Sequence presented in this particular order? This way, it allows us to experience the fullest benefits of this God-devised design. Each element builds on the one before it, creating an amazing synergy that is more than any one of the elements alone. Accessing and experiencing faith opens us up more fully, so that we can then support the presence of hope, which allows for our fullest love reception, which in turn, helps us to gain and grant charity. Now let's explore these four amazing gifts more deeply.

Faith

Faith, as the first element, could be thought of as unconditional trust, which opens the door so that we can receive other gifts. This means that faith is a quality that exists and is experienced before we ever take any action. Faith does not merely exist because of what outcome it may bring. The backward logic of our primitive brain would only have faith if the plan worked, making faith an after-the-fact condition—which is really no faith.

Unconditional trust translates into faith that the Divine will always provide, if we allow and accept the offerings. This faith also means that we trust that the One will provide, and that these offerings will always and only be what we need and how we need them. If we hold a preconceived notion about what and how we need things to exist in our life, we only limit the unlimited creativity of the universe.

I'll relate a brief story here that taught me about the place that *precedes* trust. I arranged an opportunity to take a walk with what indigenous people call a shaman. This wise man was tuned into the ever-present Spiritual Energy that communicates through everything and everyone. He guided me on a walk through the woods so that I could also make more of a connection through communicating with nature.

This shaman walked with me, asking me to stop along our path to just sense, observe, and feel the environment, whether water, trees, plants, insects, or birds. At one point along our walk, he asked me to stop and step into this large bush, explaining it was a horsetail bush. Now I'd done something like this in the past. I'd noticed how trusting plants and trees must be, to just grow and bloom without worry about their size, shape, or anything, for that matter.

I cleared my prejudiced mind and opened my heart as I stood communing with this horsetail bush. Soon I found that I was connecting with this bush and was escorted to a place of being that I call "the place before trust." I realized that trust is a word, a concept we create here on earth, to provide some sense of security *after* we feel disconnected from Source.

Faith or unconditional trust acts as something to hold on to in the dark of felt separation from Source. However, the truth is that disconnecting is not possible. There exists an inseparable oneness with Source, making trust an irrelevant concept. In a way, in this place of inseparable Oneness, faith also ceases—as does hope, love, and charity, since need ceases as well. The four qualities are not necessary in Oneness. They exist outside of oneness, providing us with a pathway back to Source.

Knowing the destination, we'll continue traveling as guided by our map. Flexibility comes into play with faith so that we remain open to all possibilities. Patience also resides here so we can remain open without jumping to conclusions. Foresight helps us look ahead to see, knowing what the outcome might be if we become overly eager and give in to our primitive brain impulses.

Faith happens for the experience of ongoing faith itself, not for the outcome. Notice the relief of letting go in faith that moves us closer to union. Extending this to God, self, others, and the universe allows us optimum access to infinite generosity. To experience faith toward God allows us to trust that what this Being provides is always coming from unconditional love. Open, surrender, and receive.

Faith toward ourselves then allows us to utilize this infinite bounty. When we trust ourselves, we gain access to our instincts and intuition. This connection to our instincts and intuition provides us with uncanny skills to navigate through life. Some might call this trust in oneself confidence. That's another word for the same opening to the infinite self and the Infinite Source.

Second only to faith in the Divine, faith in self provides a reconnection to our inner gyroscope and our personal gifts. This inner knowing also provides us with a safe place from which to discern when others are truly trustworthy. Our gut instinct becomes loud and clear. We attain comfort and safety knowing that the Divine is the infinite Source, and that no person, place, or thing can provide, dilute, or remove what only God grants us.

As we extend faith to God and to ourselves, we can notice how we alter within as we take stock of ourselves. Perhaps our sense of security is increased, knowing that God puts that much faith in us as we place full faith in God. Security is no longer based on what is happening around us; it becomes a permanent presence from within. Placing full faith in ourselves changes how we interact with others.

Other people no longer hold what we need for our sense of worth or security, regardless of how much or how little faith they place in us. Notice how the old backward thinking reverses. The tables are turned; we now choose carefully and then place faith in others, watching them bloom and flourish just as we did. Instead of trying to collect or acquire faith, we now become faith distributors. Giving and receiving faith from the Infinite Source provides us amazing immunity.

Faith toward the universe follows this faith in God, self, and others. Faith in the universe means that we trust the information we receive from the universe through the Law of Reflection. We learn to understand these symbolic messages. The Universe never lies or misleads us. We just need to place our full faith in the universe with an absence of need for how things *should* be in our lives.

Once acknowledging how things truly are in life, no matter how much we don't like it, we can make changes for the better from this point. Faith in the universe also means that we trust that all things tangible and intangible exist, therefore, everything that we need already exists. We just clear our awareness with faith, then we find what we need.

Here is another simple universal law: solutions exist *before* problems. Think back to a problem in your past that you solved; it could be anything from a math problem to a personal one. Notice that the solution you found was something that already existed.

Even if you came up with something new, a hybrid of sorts, the ingredients used for this creative solution already existed in some way. This pre-existing solution principle is always present, since everything already exists in this universe. Your point of view and awareness allow you to discover this again and again. Notice this, and take comfort in it.

Hope

Hope naturally follows faith, and may be considered a belief in all things being possible. Since all elements already exist, hope opens us up to remembering, noticing, and utilizing the infinite generosity applied to God, self, others, and the universe.

Hope toward God translates into a feeling of comfort and optimism. Notice the feeling that hope brings us. By truly immersing ourselves in hope, we can feel our beings expand and lighten. No longer feeling constricted and heavy, we feel released from the bonds of our brains. Our hearts and spirits remember the truth of the original relationship with the One. The wishful thinking of our brains is replaced by a knowing and feeling of hope. Hope becomes truth rather than wish.

Backward thinking tried to convince us to let go of hope when things did not work out in the past. Our brains let go of hope, almost blaming it for or at least associating it with some sort of past failure. *A lot of good it did to hope*, we might think.. However, with the brain, hope is a bit like faith—we only believe in these qualities after the fact, and only if things went the way our ego desired. Hoping from our hearts, not our brains, is one of the ways we make it through dark times.

Hope toward God provides a sort of flotation device, telling us that while we may not see or know the answers, they do exist—and we will find them. It is all too easy for us to make poor choices and self-inflict harm when we lose hope. Hope reminds us that we don't have to go it alone in this life. God is infinite.

When we remain open and hopeful, we will find what we need most. Notice how faith works with hope; we trust we will find just what we need, and it will be uniquely suited for us. Hope keeps our eyes open, while faith is the flashlight.

Patience, foresight, and flexibility accompany hope as well. We don't become overly eager and force-fit something where it does not work as a solution. Hope allows us to hold out. We can wait while we trust and maintain hope, so that the best fit comes along.

Foresight lets us look into the future to determine if our hoped-for solution fits well into our future and overall purpose. Flexibility allows us to adjust and adapt, so we can find and use unexpected solutions. We patiently maintain faith that this best fit takes our whole being and our best future into account. Hope opens the door and invites in this best fit.

Hope extended to ourselves reminds us that when we experience hope toward the Divine, we naturally activate an awareness of hope in ourselves. How can we not extend hope to ourselves, when we realize the effect of hope toward God? Notice the fullness felt within when experiencing hope toward God. Now notice how this hope connects you to God, providing access to the infinite. Hope brings this connection to life.

Hope in ourselves helps us to recognize the internal source of hope, rather than the precarious and fleeting hope we may receive from some other person or something we supposedly do to verify reasons for hope. Just like faith, hope exists for the sake of hope; it is an always available energy, with no beginning or end.

Though we do not always know the answers to our searches, hope lets us know that answers exist and that these answers stem from God. At a time in my past when I really wanted to let go of hope, a voice from within told me to continue on, as though some day this would all matter. I kept and nurtured all of my gifts until later I found how they fit into my life.

Hope extended toward others lets us take a deeper look into them, to see and sense the spiritual being residing within. Now, of course I don't suggest that you be so naïve as to subject yourself to known criminals and expect to experience their spiritual being. However, with the vast majority of the population, when we extend hope toward them it helps awaken them to their own positive possibilities.

Sometimes people just forget about hope, or circumstances in their life distract them. Providing a ray of hope for others to see can revive them. Have you ever noticed how folks come alive when they hope again? You know that energy, right? When we fill with hope to God and ourselves, we just naturally extend this overflow toward others. Nobody can take your hope, but you sure can share it to light a fire in others.

Hope toward the universe connects us with the larger whole of the infinite. Here we commune with the All, and realize how we are permanently okay and safe in the larger spiritual sense. With hope toward the universe, the feeling of aloneness that is so easy to come by on this earth vanishes. Hope almost becomes something more than hope itself, when we sense this universal unity. Perhaps hope simply becomes truth again.

Love

We add to our experience of the third quality, love, when we experience faith and hope, which come first to pave the way for the richest experience of love. These preceding qualities allow us to open ourselves, expanding our beings and experiencing love to the fullest with God, self, others, and the universe.

Love may be the most sought after and cherished treasure of all. As William Law stated, "Love has no errors, for all errors are the want for love." No matter how far-fetched and misguided the effort may seem, we are trying to either obtain love or keep it.

Notice the mad dash and frantic search for love in the world, and the reactions to feeling it has been lost. Addicts, self-abusers, abusers of others, the relentlessly driven, and dropouts are all like the rest of us in that we each long for lasting love. We just let our brains or traumatized selves do the searching, and they overlooked the Source.

Love toward God uses the foundation of faith and hope to provide a pathway for receiving this love from God. It just automatically happens when we extend love toward God, unconditional love; we instantly realize the utmost of unconditional love from God. Amazing! The backward logic that God loves you after you love God is simply not true. Love from God-Source exists as unconditional, remaining present with us regardless of our feelings toward God.

We notice this love from the Divine more fully when we extend unconditional love toward God. When you open your arms to embrace more fully, notice how much more you can also receive. We discover the awareness that this love was present all along, similar to what happens when we extend unconditional trust and belief in all possibilities. We get to let go of trivial conditions, meaningless distractions, and old burnt-out grudges. We come again to realize the incredible purity of this original love, and the transformation within that happens as it washes over us.

Several things come to be known in the midst of experiencing of this love toward God and the love from God. We can realize the permanence of this love connection and original nature of this relationship, along with our original pure nature. All slights and injuries that we thought we incurred along the way were only from other humans who did not know love. The original relationship with God is not interfered with or in any way compromised. We remember the One Truth.

Our brain's way of reasoning is to blame God for our misunderstanding or for events that hurt us in our life. But God neither made that other hurtful person act, nor was necessarily supposed to stop them. Free will and that other person's intense emotional pain is what led the individual to take it out on us.

This hurtful person simply made a transfer of energy, trying to decrease his or her pain by giving some to another person. We then detected and internalized some of their pain, mistaking it for our own. Your Spirit-self can bring your wounded human self to a place of the healing One Truth.

Love toward God provides a sort of protective coating of the Divine's love around us. This surrounding love informs us of our spiritual nature, our pure beauty, and that our spirit cannot be touched or harmed by a human. The more we connect with Divine Love, the safer, more secure, and peaceful we become from the inside as we know our Source.

Charity

Charity becomes a natural extension of faith, hope, and love. Charity exists as a sort of forgiveness, a release of stored unpleasant emotions and negative energy. How can we forgive and release, if we still need to experience love? This reasoning is why charity comes after faith, hope, and love.

So—we start with charity toward God, huh? Why does God need charity? I imagine that most of us, at one time or another (myself included) felt angry toward God and blamed this being for what happened to us. We blamed someone we loved, or we felt anger toward God for what did *not* happen for us. This anger at God is natural, and most of us pass through this point.

Some people, however, get bogged down at the point of anger, limiting their relationship with the Divine from that point forward. Faith, hope, and love toward the Divine become diminished. In particular, faith toward the Divine opens our heart to the Divine. However, when we get angry, our heart closes. We then limit what we receive and isolate ourselves. Life becomes more problematic when we feel and live this way, in self-deprivation. We then add another layer of anger at God, because things are going worse. Our awareness is the moving part.

This anger toward God usually just reflects our lack of knowledge about God and the universe that is God. We blame, or at least our inverted logic brains blame, God for what we don't understand. Don't get me wrong; I don't understand it either. I just know that there's more to God and the universe than I can fathom, and that living a four times four life feels and works better. Plus, I get out of my brain traps, which were the actual source of my perceived limitations.

In order to extend charity toward God, we must first acknowledge our own ignorance and the rage born of this. We take responsibility for our own creations of any thoughts, emotions, or actions that led to or stemmed from our anger. Once we own these creations, we begin to experience the first step toward freedom that charity allows.

We take back our thoughts, feelings, and actions that expressed our anger at God, and then we extend charity forward from a new perspective. We acknowledge that we did not understand, and that we felt fear and longing. Notice how faith and hope provide a bridge to God; we acknowledge our confusion, then clear the way to truly express charity toward God, releasing our own pent-up distress. This release grants us freedom.

It soon becomes clear that forgiveness is an internal act that allows us to release mental and emotional pain. This whole experience of being angry with God took place inside ourselves. Therefore, we now recognize the need to forgive ourselves for holding these pointless grudges that only limited us.

This charity toward the self also comes into play when we identify what we consider emotional hurts from other people. We held these emotions and limited ourselves, when we were actually the ones who generated and held these emotions. Beyond the initial offense by another person, the emotional pain that follows is self-inflicted.

Now, before you get angry with me, take a moment and honestly search within and observe.

Since this person disengaged with you, whether it was minutes or years ago, the distress came from a particular perspective that granted this offender control over your thoughts and emotions and self-concept—reversed logic at its worst. I don't claim the release and reclamation of the self to be easy, but it can be done. Your Spirit-self can release what your brain imposed on you.

There is no fault, blame, or outside culprit in this process, and most importantly, charity means *not blaming yourself*. Thankfully, we each have private access to our misunderstandings. We alone generate and are masters of the process that our brain misled us into as a supposed solution. Somehow, we came to believe that by holding the festering emotional hurts, we could recover. Backward, isn't it? What we hold on to and what we let go of in this life may be among the most significant decisions we make.

Now we move to a potentially very powerful aspect of charity. Whatever hurts we have held inside ourselves—the thoughts, emotions, and general painful energy—become the primary antagonist to our human system. This harbored anger, fear, sadness, or other painful emotion poses a danger to our mental, emotional, physical, and spiritual wellbeing.

Reversed reasoning, the illusion makers, told us to treat these emotional wounds as real and accurate statements about our worth. We further trap these wounds and disempower ourselves by believing that somehow, the offender must take these wounds away. Forgiveness is a release of what we never needed to hold in the first place; forgiveness is for and of the self. Tracing back from the supposed outside source of the emotional wound, we find a reversal of misfortune.

It turns out that our primitive-brain decision to hold on to the illusions about our lack of worth is the source of our prolonged pain. We forgive ourselves for our own primitive-brain error, and experience what we long to feel in the first place. The primitive brain may not be able to forgive, because it tends to use primitive-brain logic. Your spiritual self in the place of the One Truth knows better, and more.

Once we realize that we have accidentally been misled by our primitive brain into holding these negative energies, we release them through charity toward ourselves. This release extends down into the deepest aspects of our beings, just as the painful energies had extended to the same depth. Upon reaching higher consciousness, we realize that we did not mean to hold these pains. We just misunderstood what to do, and our human reflexes took over. Now, understanding this from a higher place, compassion rushes in to fill and soothe.

We recognize that we no longer need to hold these limiting energies. Now, we can feel within our being and sense a clearing at the cellular level. We truly experience charity, releasing the pent-up energy that was the only antagonist to our system in the first place.

Feel the limiting energy fade and evaporate. The flood of faith, hope, and love saturates our being at every level, reminding us of our God-created nature as we give thanks, remembering the One Truth.

Charity toward others is guided by realizing that no matter what people say or do to us, their behavior only reveals their inner perspectives, wounds, needs, values, and beliefs. Their choice only tells us about them—nothing about ourselves. Remember the paint chip example here. Once we stop the primitive-brain reflexes of egocentricity, generalizing, transductive logic, and the rest, we free ourselves.

Charity naturally leads to a sense of true freedom as we release ourselves and others from the captivity imposed by harbored resentment. Once free, we can let others go free, since they are no longer a threat. In this case, charity represents a kind of prevention of primitive-brain traps.

Charity toward the universe naturally occurs upon giving this to God, self, and others. We grant this forgiveness as we come to understand that our environment and the universe as a whole is not conspiring against us. The earth and nature have their own processes to go through. Our new awareness about the universe and our environment removes any sense of prejudice either from ourselves or from the universe. Animals and other aspects of nature no longer pose a threat beyond practical precautions.

With love in place within our hearts and beings, we can release the pent-up bitterness we had kept in storage since it was oddly retained, only awaiting love. We just misunderstood the source of the solution. We held these old hurts because at some level we believed these other people would or could provide what only God can—unconditional love.

The painful restrictions produced by holding the hurt—insult to injury—can be released. This is why charity and forgiveness start with God and then move to self, for unnecessarily holding the hurts in the first place. Is there anything left to forgive, after we release and remember the One Truth?

Now, extending charity out into our future, imagine starting each day with charity so that we don't accumulate these hurts we might encounter in everyday life. "Fore-giving," as in future forgiving, allows us to stay clear within, remaining in the One Truth and the immunity it grants.

As I continue working with these four states of faith, hope, love and, charity, I find an interesting phenomenon occurs. When reaching the highest state of consciousness, the place of oneness, faith and hope cease to exit. It seems that these two states serve as ladders to or reminders of oneness.

The opposite experience happens to love and charity when in the highest consciousness. Love and charity strengthen and expand to the point of overflowing from within to all of humanity.

Try this yourself. Access your highest state. Merge into it and experience it fully. What becomes of faith and hope? What becomes of love and charity? Notice the relationship and dynamics between the highest consciousness and these four states.

CHAPTER 8

WAYS OF EXPERIENCING THE ONE TRUTH

You have travelled a great distance to this point. Starting with your primitive brain, going into the land of illusions and back out again, you find a clearing. Your dedication and determination, along with allowing new awareness, bring you to this collection of exercises. Here you will find methods designed to promote reconnecting and remembering your Divine nature. You can carry these tools with you throughout your life, using them whenever you feel out of sorts or out of touch with the Truth.

This chapter includes several ways for you to experience the One Truth. Each of the exercises here will guide you through your consciousness to a higher level, where you can connect with the One Truth. Notice what happens and what you find with each exercise. You will reach a place of awareness that is not new, just a return to your Sacred Nature.

Quite a Stretch

You could think of this exercise as peripheral vision for your spirit. Expanding your awareness breaks you free from the confines and consequences of survival mode. Start by noticing your inner self, just sensing and observing how you feel within your body. Now expand this awareness to beyond your body, approximately one foot larger. Notice the sensations with this and how you feel here.

Next, let your awareness expand to fill the room. Take a moment to do this and then notice the sensations you experience with this and how you feel. Now expand to the entire building and notice the feeling. With each of these next expansion levels, just take a moment and observe what you experience and how you feel. Now expand as large as your city, your state, your country, continent, hemisphere, planet, solar system, galaxy, and then infinity. Sense and observe.

This expansion exercise plays on what I consider the dynamics of energy. We exist as energy. Our awareness is the only moving part in our experience. Yes, I know, energy is never static; it's always moving. However, moving our awareness provides us with more to notice of what is already perpetual motion.

What we notice is not new—only our awareness of it. With each expansion we become more aware, noticing more over time, with certain resulting sensations and feelings. We'll bypass the physics discussion about the effects of observation, since this takes us into territory outside our focus. What matters here is what we do with our awareness and free will.

Straight Through the Heart

I experienced the effects of this process during a workshop presented by Russ Hudson on enneagrams. I found it so heart-opening that I share it with my clients, and now with you. This exercise consists of a single question, repeated maybe twenty to thirty times.

The question invites you to connect with your heart and simply describe the experience. You may discover a different answer each time. You may get some repeats, and you may even experience some blanks (a void of sorts).

There are no wrong answers, just whatever you find.

The question is: What do you experience when you are more present with your heart? Let this question invite you to connect with your heart and simply feel and experience. Say aloud what you experience. Then just ask again, saying it aloud, and continue asking twenty to thirty times, or for about five minutes.

What I find is that this question helps me lose my small self and connect with my infinite self, my Spirit-self. I also find that it provides me with a way into the Sacred Sequence, as I begin noticing a natural Divine Order. I receive what I find in my heart, and naturally express this outwardly.

Rising Above Yourself: The Words and Colors of the Infinite Eternal)

With this experience, we climb the ladder of consciousness to reach the One Truth. We each possess layers of consciousness. These correspond to the levels of human development. What intrigues me about this innate layering, from the perspective of a counselor with a doctorate in human development counseling, is that we already possess the necessary ingredients to function from a higher level.

The difference in our level of functioning stems from two main aspects. We must overcome trauma and come to recognize that we already possess these levels of consciousness. The levels provide a pathway that ascends to grant connection with the One Source. The key here is that we *can* learn how to use what we innately possess.

This process of rising above yourself is based on the work of Michael Hall, PhD, a clinical psychologist who identified a method of accessing higher states of consciousness called "meta-stating."™ With meta-stating, you start with a currently active emotional state—pleasant or unpleasant— and use this as the basis to ascend.

To start, just connect inside yourself and observe how you feel emotionally. Notice any emotions without judging them. Just identify one or more—curiosity, for example, or maybe some anxiety. Second, notice where you experience this emotion in your body. Every emotion expresses itself in your body with some kind of sensation, such as tightness, heaviness, or an effervescence or lightness, among many others. Notice how your emotion announces itself in your body.

We'll go through the scenario using unpleasant and pleasant emotions as the first step, starting with the unpleasant one—be it anxiety, sadness, or an anger variation. Once you identify and sense this emotion within your body, imagine placing this energy outside of your body. Allow this emotional energy to form into an image: a symbol that represents the emotion. Whatever person, place, thing or color comes to mind is perfect. My clients often find that unpleasant emotions appear as dark, dense blobs.

With the unpleasant energy outside you, what emotion do you experience in the place where the other was located? Maybe this is relief, calm or something similar. For those of you who started with a pleasant emotion, you can join in the process in the next paragraph with your emotion.

Connect with the emotion and its physical sensation. Experience and feel it. Imagine that you put this emotion on a dial, then turn it all the way up to the fullest so that you experience relief to the absolute utmost. What do you find here, and what do you call it? Maybe it is something like calm, peace, or relaxation. Notice the physical sensations with this emotion, and just experience them all.

The next step is simply to turn up this new emotion to the fullest. So if it is calm, imagine that calm to the absolute utmost. What does this become, and what do you call it? Maybe you find peace, joy, or something else. There are no wrong answers existing in this unique journey. Just notice, name, and experience the energy and sensations.

Now turn this new emotion up to the fullest, letting go and opening up to whatever is the next layer. Maybe you find some emotion like bliss, joy or love. Feel this emotion and notice the way your body feels along with it. You may find, at this level or the next, that you run out of words to describe the emotion or the awareness. This brings us to the place beyond words—pure awareness.

Your mind may represent this as a color—maybe light blue, yellow, or white. Just notice and receive this color. What do you feel in your physical self, as this color infuses and fills your being? Notice how this color is infinite. You may also find that, as this beautiful color saturates you from within that it changes a bit. It may go from light blue to white, for example.

Sometimes you find that there is one small notch up in consciousness.

Whether you stay with the color that infuses you or it alters a bit after infusing, this is the place of One Truth—your place of pure awareness and effortless being. You just *are*—and you just receive, fully merging with Source or God. You can notice the Sacred Sequence acts as a support structure to keep you in the One Truth.

From here, observe what you find to be true about yourself. Maybe you find that you simply exist in a pure state, infused with love from the Divine. From there, glance at any old limiting belief about the self or life generated by the primitive brain. Observe a situation in which you felt worry, anger, sadness. How does this look now, from this place of the One Truth? This Truth about your being existed before your birth, and will exist after your death; it is truly eternal. As you feel this, you know nothing on this earth can affect this Truth. This Truth is not of this earth.

If you see a color or figure that represents this highest consciousness, this Truth, let this Infinite Source then infuse into that unpleasant emotion (the blob or whatever you see) residing outside of you. Simply observe as this Infinite Energy infuses and saturates, transforming the old. What happens, and what do you feel?

Let yourself stay in the place of One Truth—receiving, feeling, experiencing. Notice what you feel in your physical self. You may find that aches and pains are either lessened or gone entirely. Notice what happens with your energy. It may now be a smooth flow: comfortable, yet fully enabled. It is interesting how in the One Truth there are no questions, just pure being. Questions actually break you out of the One. The primitive brain asks questions, while Spirit-self basks in the One.

Please visit this state often, especially at the start and end of your day, to remember and set the tone for your phases of waking and sleeping.

Loving Our Shadows into the Light

The process described here is based on the work of Carl Jung, as well as some of internal family systems concepts developed by Dr. Richard Schwartz, in addition to my own experiences in personal growth work. I find this particular method quite profound, since it reaches parts of ourselves long shunned to let us discover deeply satisfying gifts. It really utilizes the Sacred Sequence, which you'll notice after going through this exercise for yourself.

How do we create a shadow, and how does our shadow affect us? First of all, volumes of material about our shadows have been written. I will provide a very brief overview from a practical perspective. Then we'll learn how to work with our shadow to re-integrate the segregated part of the self.

For the purpose of this work, our shadow exists as a part of the self that was judged and rejected by a significant other person, usually in childhood. As a result of the illusion makers, we come to believe that this part of the self endangers our lives. As a survival instinct, we also reject this part of ourselves. We separate a part or parts of the self, and our shadow is born.

We withhold love from the part of ourselves that came into existence as a result of experiencing rejection. We reject our shadow part, trying to deny that it exists, or push it away. That's a primitive-brain response, for sure. How can the denial of love solve what the absence of love caused?

The significant dynamic of a shadow here is that it is a part of the self that was rejected by the *self*, after experiencing rejection by a significant other person. However, the surprise in this shadow world is that this part remains dedicated to us, just as it was when it was integrated in our whole being.

The shadow remains in loving service to us to keep us safe—not to attack or harm us. This shadow part is actually always dedicated and in service to us, but goes about this in a different way when part of the positive whole.

My belief is that the shadow is restricted to negative or dark communication due to its separation from the positive light of the whole, original self. Shadow is rigid in form and function, since it is a product of the primitive brain. No prodding or efforts to persuade it will make it change. Many traditional approaches to working with the shadow involve understanding what benefits it has to offer, leading to some modification in the relationship. But here we are seeking to understand and love our shadow into freedom and light.

The trauma and splintering process seems to invert the part that is split off. The inversion takes the form of negative self-talk since this part is separated from the whole. This shadow language requires translating. The negative message is actually a call to develop the self, and the qualities that are lagging behind the rest of the self.

We try our best to suppress this supposedly dangerous part of the self. We may deny we possess this quality at all. We may find that we can only allow ourselves to notice it in others, and dislike them for what we can't allow in ourselves.

For example, we can't allow ourselves to gain recognition from others, so we feel jealousy toward those who can permit this recognition. We can't allow ourselves to assert the self or express anger directly, so we restrict ourselves to passive or passive-aggressive actions.

One of the dangers of life after splitting is that the person just focuses on the aspects of the self that are free, which only makes it easier to avoid the shadow. The primitive brain feels satisfied with this approach, until shadow breaks through in some troublemaking way.

In order to survive a trauma, we usually take one of two strategies: We either turn up some personal quality, or turn it down. For example, assertive becomes aggressive, or confidence becomes arrogance. Sharing becomes hoarding, possessions or money.

We may turn down a quality so that assertive becomes passive, or low confidence becomes that voice in your head that says you're not good enough. Sharing would turn into giving it all away. The choice of whether to turn some quality up or down depends on what the person believes will better lead to his or her own survival. This splintering leads to qualities with limited abilities.

Let's say a child attempts to assert herself to her parents, and is met with harsh punishment. She must then reject assertiveness and aggressiveness as response options, unless she wants to face what feels like death. Her shadow becomes assertiveness and aggressiveness. If she even comes close to assertive expression of self, it feels like it is life threatening. Her ever-protective shadow part tells her so.

Another child learns to increase her assertiveness and overpower her parents with her aggressiveness. Her shadow becomes assertiveness and passiveness. Her ever-protective shadow tells her she must always act aggressively or else risk extinction, or at least helplessness.

The survival mechanism of over- or under-developing the self is still subject to shadow influence. When the original quality of what is now shadow would be needed, it is not available. Over- or under-developing some aspect of the self, driven by ego, attempts to compensate for the loss of the shadow part. The more compensating that occurs, the more compensation is needed, because it never reaches the deeper need; it just works around it. A passive or aggressive person will end up not meeting their need to feel worthy of love. But they will continue the pattern anyway, often exaggerating the trait even more in response to frustrated needs. Thus, a sort of addiction process is set in motion until the shadow is accessed and loved.

What we dislike in ourselves is actually present out of pure, dedicated love, for our protection. This part that protects us—the painful emotions, beliefs, and restricted behavior—lasts until we can show and share Divine Love with this part of ourselves. The beliefs about the self and qualities about the self that we hate possess a loving devotion to us that is beyond description. This part protects us until we have enough awareness and ability to do what we were unable to, do at the time of the trauma.

Only by receiving this pure, Divine Love and then showing the capacity to share it within—rather than continuing to judge and reject the undesirable part of the self—do we gain our release. The Sacred Sequence is applied within so that we receive from God, then extend from what the self receives to others. In this case, others represent our shadow. Once convincing the shadow that we are able to receive and share this Love within, it either transforms into an ally, or simply transforms and vanishes from us.

Again, outward displays and symptoms are distractions from the true source of resolution. We gain re-entry through the outermost layer of the trauma, going back into the true source. Symptoms simply exist as the outermost consequence of how we cope with trauma.

By tracing the outward signs back to the coping, we gain access to the original trauma. By bringing the focus of the resolution back inside the self, we can then bypass the temptation to judge the self for these "misbehaviors." Understanding what led to and motivated the transgressions provides compassion and excludes judgment.

Resolution comes when we show that we can love—truly, unconditionally love—and share this with the shadow, understanding that this shadow was a teacher, a protector, and encourager in service to us. We may have previously withheld love from our shadows, consequently prolonging the separation.

The resolution involves understanding of the shadow and its purpose, as well as its loving, dedicated role. Until you understand it, feel compassion for its selfless function, and love it, it will remain a shadow. However, once understanding, compassion, and loving occur, the shadow then knows you have developed to the point where it is no longer necessary. You have mastered the skills needed to break free from within, so the shadow transforms.

The resolution does not involve the actual traumatic event outside of the self, unless it is necessary if we wish to understand it, or if it might help diffuse the belief-perception system that birthed the shadow. It also does not involve working to overcome fear of the shadow so that we can gradually incorporate the shadow into daily life. On the other hand, the resolution does involve understanding the purpose of the shadow and its function, and appreciating its incredible love and dedication, its act of pure love for us.

When we come to understand our shadow's undying service to us, then give it compassion and love, our shadow yields and transforms. Once accessing our evolved consciousness and demonstrating this to our shadow, its work is done. This reviled part of us, born of rejection, actually serves to keep us safe until we reach a point in our consciousness that allows us to recognize and reach its core of love. Shadow and the larger self can then reunite as allies.

Shadow may limit us or impulsively move us into some behavior, but either way, the shadow performs its service to protect us. Shadow does not consider the big picture—just immediate safety. The threat is all that matters, not the consequence of the chosen strategy to maintain safety.

Self-defeating behavior reveals the shadow, as does our inner dialogue just before a self-defeating act. The dialogue may include self-talk about inabilities and inferiorities, or point our personal limitations to avoid endangering the self.

Shadow devotes itself in love to keeping the larger self safe. Of course, during these times of self-defeating behavior, we just want to reject the shadow that much more. Understanding its devotion and love for us will aid in bringing this shadow into the light. Then we can rediscover the self.

Here is the Sacred Sequence, the four elements flowing from God to self to others, the "inner other" which is shadow, and then the universe as outward constructive expression. We can then display the abilities that the shadow needs to see and feel faith, hope, love, and charity. This transforms, integrates, or simply blends shadow into the light. In an odd way, shadow was waiting for us to develop enough to access and share these elements in this order. Now its work is done.

Consider an additional perspective here about our shadow aspects. Some physicists speculate that the universe exists in a hologram structure; this means that any part of the whole contains the same structure as the whole. Dr. David Bohm is a key developer of this point of view.

Now apply this hologram concept to ourselves and our shadows. This means that God resides within us at our core. With this being the case, each of our shadow parts also retains a core of pure Divine Energy. Know this and take comfort in it, as you look at any and all of your shadow parts. No matter how ugly they may seem on the surface, at their core is pure love, exactly like yours! The concept of namaste not only applies to other people, but also to our shadow!

Below you will find the step-by-step process for loving your shadow into the light.

1. Identify a way in which you overdo or underdo, deprive or overindulge. This may reveal a shadow. Notice the emotion that comes with the over- or underdoing. This may provide an opening to the disowned part that asks for recovery. Emotions associated with shadows tend to be in the forms of anger, sadness, or anxiety.

2. Once you identify the over-under aspect and the emotions that come with it, you can then connect with the emotional energy within yourself, in your body. Feel this and notice where in your body this energy resides—chest, stomach, shoulders, etc.

3. Create an opportunity to reconcile with the disowned part of the self. Let this energy emerge from within and take some shape or form. Allow your loving heart to delve down into the deepest layer of this energy, which appears on the surface as anger, sadness, or anxiety.

4. Connect with the core of the external energy and locate its heart. What emotion do you find here? How does it respond to you discovering and acknowledging it? How do you feel now, knowing its heart and true feelings toward you?

5. Notice and feel this relationship. Commune until reconciled and integrated; enjoy the new you, looking into your life to find the ways this fuller you will express.

Describe the process of identifying the emotional behavior and belief. Find its function: the obvious aspect that we dislike. Then identify the subtle part that is what it protects you from, and how it protects you through incredible unyielding dedication. In some ways, the goal of the shadow is to prevent us from experiencing emotional hurt.

Why does it actually seem to inflict the very pain you want to avoid? It isn't inflicting; rather, it reveals our developmental limitations. After this, some softening may occur just by understanding its purpose, and the loving dedication that holds it in place post-trauma.

The next step is accessing Divine Love. Fill and feel this within the larger self, then share the Infinite Source with this part and notice, observe, and experience the altering. What changes do you see, and how does it integrate this love? Now an ally with a new style and mission, this formerly disliked and rejected part serves a vital yet similar function in service of love for us.

As an additional application of this loving your shadow work, identify a quality that you wish you had. This may be self-respect, for example. Maybe you wish for courage or motivation—but for what reason and what purpose? To find the desired quality, identify the shadow aspect of the self, since we each get access to All.

The shadow is the opposite of the quality you desire. Self-respect brings a shadow of disregard for the self and one's wellbeing. Courage shows you a shadow of fear, while motivation reveals one of indifference or complacency. Keep in mind that shadow blocks you for your own safety and protection. Again, love the purpose of your shadow, understand it, and give it compassion and love to activate and apply this quality. This process can happen by applying the five steps of loving your shadow into the light.

Reclaiming Yourself

This exercise was presented in another chapter, in the example with James and his self-confidence. I present this exercise again here to give you the full collection of healing exercises in one place.

It sure seems easy in this life to feel that somehow, something is missing. And maybe that something feels a bit like happiness, peace, satisfaction, or a similar emotion. At the same time, it is also easy to experience a repeated feeling of one of the three primary emotions: fear, anger, or sadness. These emotions may activate during certain similar situations in your life.

And while you may seek to get rid of the uncomfortable emotions and replace them with the comfortable, it is not as simple as just choosing to shift. You experience the uncomfortable emotions as a signal, or a wake-up call, to interpret the language so that you can access and heal the wound.

Translating the uncomfortable emotion and its associated belief about the self, as well as accessing the wound and bringing healing, is the purpose of this exercise. In general, what might be considered healing may really just be the act and consequence of reclaiming lost parts of the self.

These lost parts may act as shadows, but also as vacancies: a noticeable lack of something. The absence of this lost quality could be considered a vague, subtle shadow rather than the more overt presence of a true shadow quality that actively expresses itself. Lost parts seem lost because they are lost to us.

What is missing? It is common to disconnect from one or more aspects of the self in response to trauma. These lost parts of the self may include traits such as self-trust being replaced by doubt.

It's interesting to note that when people lose self-trust, they often display incredible blind trust, deferring helplessly to others, which only leads to further disappointment. Then the person vows never to trust anyone, ever again. As we know, recovery is an inside job. It is the inner relationship with the self that provides the ability to know whom you really can and cannot trust.

In this exercise, we'll access and use the ways that your brain symbolically encodes and represents experiences and emotions. These symbols used by the brain to stand for events and emotions may be colors or icons that include a myriad of perspectives and emotions. Think of these icons as similar to the symbols used in dreams. Do not let your literal-thinking primitive brain interfere with this exercise. The primitive brain can observe and reap the benefits.

One of the challenges to reclaiming lost parts of the self includes the concept of forgiveness. We may find that, in the process of accessing a lost part, we encounter anger at the person we believe took this part from us. This traumatic incident provides a very powerful opportunity for the Spirit-self to correct what the primitive brain misunderstands. Some might call this correction a shift from third-dimensional thinking to fourth-dimensional thinking, converting the third dimension into the fourth.

As stated earlier, we tend to hold on to our traumatic experiences. The reasoning is that the remnant can somehow be useful or converted into redemption. However, only Truth is redeeming; the trauma remnant simply occupies a place that Truth can heal.

Holding what hurts keeps the healing from happening, yet the primitive brain reasons that holding it will somehow lead to healing. Furthermore, with the primitive brain's focus on threats, it seems unavoidable that it would lock its focus on the trauma to keep it from hurting.

A faint hope seems present that someone will come along and remove this traumatic wound. Yet taking away the hurt doesn't restore the lost part. *You* can initiate the process that takes it away, and restore the part of the self that was lost. However, a key toll booth that must be passed through along the way to healing is the process of forgiveness.

Forgiveness does *not* mean that what the other person did is okay. It actually has nothing to do with the other person. Forgiveness is an action we take for ourselves only! Letting go of that which hurts us is forgiving. This is a task we do within ourselves, and does not involve the offender at all. Forgiving the offender is irrelevant.

Often, forgiveness and trust get mixed in together, but these are two very separate and different processes. Sometimes we think that forgiving means we will trust the offender again. NO! Trusting the offender is not part of forgiving.

Forgiveness, Undoing the Split, and Restoring Unity

The energy you need to accomplish this process is something you already possess and know how to use. It's applying it to where you had failed to do so, or rather, where you withheld it. You can learn to do your own energy work—it's nothing mysterious; it's just love. We think and feel that our shadow is the problem, when in fact, our *response* to it is the problem. It's similar to stress, which is not an event; it's a response to an event.

Is forgiveness a process that heals the split within? Is forgiveness simply a reconciliation within the self, between parts separated by trauma? If so, then there is no blame toward the event, offender, or anyone or anything—just unity with the One Truth. This moves the process within and nullifies the primitive brain's external search for answers. This inner search provides us with answers in a time of change.

Forgiveness is the closest thing we have to undoing that which was done. Maybe it isn't just close, but is the actual undoing: it restores the aboriginal condition of Unity, the One Truth.

In the process of exploring lost parts of the self, I find a potentially powerful principle in patterns. Once recognizing that some part of the self was lost or let go of at the time of a trauma in a simple act of self-preservation, our life patterns change. Sure, we each live out patterns that tend to perpetuate themselves, reinforced just because that's what has been happening. Some patterns are constructive and beneficial, but others are destructive or harmful.

The foundation of these patterns consists partly of what we believe as true about the self and life. In addition, part of the foundation of these patterns results from personal qualities that we access or deny. Yes, this access and denial supports our beliefs, but it's a chicken-and-egg question of interdependence.

At the time of a trauma, you may let go of self-confidence, for example. This surrender also affects the sense of love-worthiness, since confidence acts as a kind of connection to the self and God. Self-confidence equates fairly well to trust of the self, which naturally leads to the Sacred Sequence qualities and the One Truth.

Let's look at the patterns and perception. Once self-confidence has been lost, we live from a deficit or lack of self-confidence, and a diminished sense of love-worthiness. This impairs our connection to God and all that connection brings. Certain choices and life patterns then come into existence.

The very powerful key here is that our primitive brain then treats these patterns, choices, and consequences as absolute truth about God, self, life, and the universe. Since the primitive brain uses a negative, fearful to look at life, it believes that patterns only exist in negative forms. Just try convincing the primitive brain that positive patterns exist, and watch the primitive brain dispute this with intense fear-based vigor.

Patterns exist in any and all forms, just like music. Placed within a great silence is a collection of sounds with a certain rhythm called music. These sounds are true within any song, and yet they do not remotely represent the infinite—simply one example.

While you may notice a life pattern, do not accept it as the only one possible, and do not think it is the way of the universe. The post-trauma choices and life patterns that develop reflect the principle that we behave according to our beliefs.

Often, it seems that we respond based on what we expect or anticipate. Manifesting anything exemplifies the general process of displaying infinite possibilities, and is not about what we specifically reveal. Reclaiming your self leads to different patterns. Let these be, and choose your song!

Now we move on to the exercise of reclaiming yourself. To start, identify a trauma in your past. Next, take stock of yourself before and after the trauma. Notice what trait or traits are missing since the trauma first occurred. As examples, you may find that due to an emotional trauma, you lack trust or confidence in yourself, assertiveness, or self-respect. Each of these traits provides important abilities and awareness, as well as making significant contributions to your wellbeing and navigation in life.

Once you identify and name a trait you feel is missing as a result of a trauma, let your mind connect with this trait. Allow your awareness to give you a symbol of some sort that represents this trait. You may find a color or some kind of icon, such as a person, place or thing, comes into your awareness. Do not reach for the symbol; just connect with the trait, the energy, and the feel of it. Hold an open space so that Source provides a symbol.

See, feel, and maybe even hear this symbol in whatever way it shows up. Now you have an image to work from, so that when you go back to the trauma scene, you will be able to find the lost part of the self. Let yourself return to the trauma scene, like you are a detective searching for a clue (the lost trait). You will notice the symbolic trait somewhere within the mental images of the event provided by your memory.

Like a homing device, let your awareness zero in on this symbol that represents the lost part of the self. Connect with this symbol and its energy in your own time and in your own way. Receive and welcome back this part of the self into your being. Feel the energy as this quality returns, informing and activating you in more complete ways. Notice how you can recover this part of the self, and how it is okay for you to keep this ability and apply it in your life. What once felt unsafe to possess now provides you with greater safety and competence. The inverted logic reverses.

You not only recover yourself, but also open up to greater self-acceptance. This self-acceptance aligns you with the Sacred Sequence. Feeling this alignment opens you to your Truth, the One Truth. Feel this as you receive, and know you can trust your ability to live this in the future, as this Truth effectively provides and guides you.

The "Thank-You Prayer

This method of prayer came to me during a time of contemplation and meditation. I began taking stock of the positives in my life. The more I gave thanks for positive people and events in my life, the more of these I found. The process seemed to reflect a life and rhythm of its own.

We can certainly discover this with a negative slant supplied by the primitive brain. In this case, I was in a higher state of consciousness and just kept noticing simple, profound positives in my life. I started with the present and went back in time, illuminating countless occasions of receiving from the Infinite's Generosity.

Once I started realizing how much I received, I simply began giving thanks to God. I noticed a gift and gave thanks, moving on to another and giving thanks. This process kept unfolding until I was in the repetitive pattern of noticing and giving thanks. I see; I thank; I see; I thank... and on and on it goes.

With each thank you, I feel it in my heart opening and receiving more and more love. This thank-you prayer is a powerful ceremony that opens and deepens your connection to the One. Unity happens through recognizing, surrender, receiving, and gratitude, which only brings more.

Keeping It Humble

In the process of our unique personal journeys of awakening and evolving, we may find amazing clarity, wonderful gifts, and incredible abilities that bring great joy. Depending on which part of the self takes stock, the primitive brain or Spirit-self, we may experience either an inflated sense of worth or grateful humility.

It seems inevitable that we will notice the place in the self that wants to lay claim to our gifts and abilities. Furthermore, while this perspective exists, it misleads us into a constrictive trap. Once we take credit for our gifts or abilities, the primitive brain steps into the driver's seat, limiting us from that point forward—or backward, as is more likely.

Personally, I remind myself that I create nothing I use in this life. I may "make" a raised bed for planting vegetables. While I assembled the materials, I did not create them; the tree created the wood.. And, even the tree knows that it simply expresses the Divine. It did not generate itself. Whether the elements are natural, synthetic, or intangible (such as words), the ingredients used to actualize anything and everything already exists. Maybe a different combination yields different results, but I *made* none of the elements.

I do use my awareness and my free will to choose, but I did not even make these abilities. I can rightly express pride in how I choose; however, it seems that only gratitude and humility fit, when it comes to what I use. Were it not for the Infinite's generosity, I would make nothing. I choose to *allow* the One who makes all things possible to live through me, and I observe the miracles.

As we conclude this chapter, let's do a brief review of this material. We now possess a collection of methods that assist in resolving traumas and remembering your Divine connection. A thread that unites each of these exercises comes in the form of the holographic universe; every part consists of the same structure as the whole. Each part of us contains a Sacred Center or God-Source, which can help dissolve our fears as we approach even our most unappealing traits.

A crucial reminder is to recognize that our first reflex to some distasteful part comes from the primitive brain. We need not use this reflex. We need not be fooled by the external surface. Knowing that whatever we perceive within ourselves or in others, we can search for and recognize the Source at the center.

The exercises in this chapter provide ways to pierce through the external to reach and re-connect with your own spiritual self. Once we become familiar with the process of reclaiming parts of the self and freeing the trapped energy, we eventually welcome the encounters with shunned aspects of self, knowing these aspects just want to come home and need our assistance to re-unite. Welcome home to yourself!

There is nothing the ripple does not reach.

AFTERTHOUGHTS

I appreciate your commitment to yourself and your own development as a person and spiritual being. I want to share a few things to consider and remember as you go forward from here.

The purpose of this book and your overall efforts is to heal from the past and evolve into your future. You can apply the concepts and exercises of this book to your past traumas. There are ways to utilize these principles to enhance your future.

You may find it helpful to start and end your day using thank-you prayer. This connects you into the Sacred Sequence and One Truth, opening your heart with loving reassurance. This can set a great tone for the day ahead, and ease you into a more restful state for overnight.

While it would be nice if we each had just one shadow, we don't. Instead, we each have many fragments of the self, floating around disconnected, yet influencing the self. Some are large shadows and others are small; some have what amounts to a few moons orbiting around them. You may find that you reclaimed and resolved some stuck parts of yourself through various exercises, including loving your shadow into the light. This awareness and skill will serve you well for the future.

You may also find that this former shadow retains some of its previous habits, and wants to respond in old ways to new situations. This initial urge to respond as before just needs to be interpreted, so that you can provide the necessary loving reassurance to your newly-integrated former shadow. You provide for it what God provides for you. Remember the gifts that your shadow brings to you for more graceful living.

Connect your love into the core of the shadow, recognizing the Divine self. Feel this as you reunite with the energy now available for constructive responses. This relationship with your shadow illustrates an inner Sacred Sequence: others are your shadow parts, rather than people.

Once you become familiar with the dynamics of shadows and the tools to bring them into the light, you can then respond effectively to any other shadow parts that declare themselves in need. You know how to translate the shadow language and the need. You also know the treasure awaiting: the resource you can access and activate back into your life. There is no need to be afraid of shadows you find in the future, because you know the process that brings them each into the light.

In closing, just remember that you are the recipient of this love-worthiness. It is you! Feel this and live from this as you go freely about your life, allowing yourself to express and create from this place of infinite, eternal sufficiency.

ABOUT THE AUTHOR, DR. JOHN BURTON

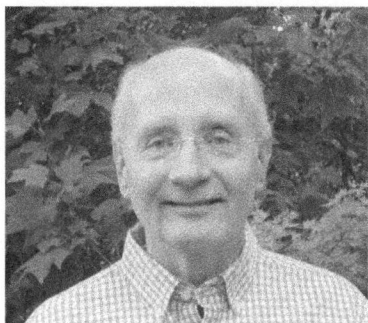

In his search for understanding human nature, Dr. John Burton completed his bachelor's in psychology, a master's in clinical psychology, and a doctorate in human development counseling. He holds licenses in South Carolina as a professional counselor and counselor supervisor, and is certified as a clinical hypnotherapist, neuro-linguistic programming master, and Reiki master.

Dr. Burton has taught at both the undergraduate and graduate levels of college, and also authored or co-authored three other books. These include *Hypnotic Language; Its Structure and Use*, co-authored with Bob Bodenhamer, D.Min. Dr. Burton is the sole author of *States of Equilibrium* and *Understanding Advanced Hypnotic Language Patterns: A Comprehensive Guide*.

He currently provides counseling and presents workshops on the Sacred Sequence and One Truth, and serves as a contributing writer for OM *Times* e-magazine, an online journal of spirituality and personal growth. Learn more about him, his workshops, and books at www.drjohnburton.com.